ENGLISH PLEASE!

English for the Arab World
Book 1

by Richard Harrison

Contents

Longman Group UK Limited,
Longman House, Burnt Mill, Harlow,
Essex CM20 2JE, England
and Associated Companies throughout the world.

First published 1994

Set in 12 on 15 pt Avant Garde

Produced by Longman Singapore Publishers Pte Ltd
Printed in Singapore

ISBN 0 582 21705 9

Introduction – To the Student

تقديم إلى الطالب

Welcome to Book 1 of *English Please!* a new English course for the Arab World.

This course consists of two books and an optional Starter Book. It is meant for those students who are new to English, or those students who know a little English, but need much more practice at basic level, especially with reading and writing.

The aims of this course are:

- to help you say and understand some useful phrases and sentences in English
- to introduce some of the grammar of the English language
- to teach you about 500 words of vocabulary (including some English words which are used in Arabic.)
- to teach you to read and write the alphabet and numbers
- to help you read and write simple sentences in English
- to help you spell words correctly and to use punctuation marks correctly
- to help you build your own list of new words and expressions

By the end of this first book you will be able to do these things in English:

- greet people and introduce yourself
- introduce friends
- talk about family and relatives
- ask people where they are from
- ask people about their jobs
- ask and give directions
- give a description of a person
- give a description of an object
- describe a street or a village
- ask to speak to someone on the phone
- ask someone to give you something
- ask the price of something

مرحباً بك معنا في الكتاب الأول English Please! ، وهو سلسلة جديدة في اللغة الإنجليزية لطلبة العالم العربي .

تتكون هذه السلسلة من كتابين، بالإضافة إلى كتاب اختياري أولي . وهي تستهدف أولئك الطلبة الذين لا يعرفون اللغة الإنجليزية، أو الذين يعرفون القليل منها، ولكنهم يحتاجون إلى التدريب الكثير على المستوى الأولي (الأساسي) خصوصاً في مهارتي القراءة والكتابة .

وتتلخص أهداف هذه السلسلة فيما يلي :

- مساعدة الطالب في أن يقول وأن يفهم بعض العبارات المفيدة، وبعض الجمل في اللغة الإنجليزية .
- تقديم بعض قواعد اللغة الإنجليزية
- تعليم الطالب عدداً من الكلمات (بما فيها الكلمات الإنجليزية التي تستخدم كما هي في العربية) .
- تعليم الطالب أن يقرأ ويكتب جملا بسيطة في اللغة الإنجليزية وبعض الأرقام .
- تعليم الطالب كيفية تهجّي بعض الكلمات بطريقة سليمة، وكذلك استخدام علامات الترقيم .
- مساعدة الطالب في تكوين قائمة بالكلمات والتعبيرات الخاصة به .

بنهاية الكتاب الأول سيتمكن التلميذ من عمل الآتي باللغة الإنجليزية :

- تحية الناس وتقديم نفسه .
- تقديم الأصدقاء .
- التحدث عن العائلة والأقارب .
- سؤال الناس عن مكان إقامتهم .
- سؤال الناس عن الوظائف .
- السؤال عن وإعطاء تعليمات (توجيهات) .
- إعطاء وصف لشخص ما .
- إعطاء وصف لشيء ما .
- وصف شارع أو قرية .
- طلب شخص على التليفون .
- طلب شيء من شخص .
- السؤال عن سعر شيء ما .

وسيستطيع الطالب أيضا أن يكتب جملا بسيطة باللغة الإنجليزية: عن نفسه، وعن عائلته، وأصدقائه، ومكان معيشته.

You will also be able to write simple sentences in English about yourself, your family and friends, and the place where you live.

وينقسم الكتاب الأول إلى هذه الأجزاء:

Book 1 is divided into these parts:

كتاب التلميذ .
كراسة الأعمال التحريرية .
الملحق .

STUDENTS' BOOK
WORKBOOK
APPENDIX

بنهاية هذه السلسلة يمكنك التخاطب مع الأجانب باللغة الإنجليزية: سواء كان أولئك الناس مثل: البريطانيين والأمريكيين الذين يتحدثون الإنجليزية كلغة أولى، أو من الجنسيات الأخرى مثل: اليابانيين والفلبينيين والسويديين والهنود الذين يتعلمون الإنجليزية كلغة ثانية، ويمكنك قراءة العلامات وكتابة الجمل البسيطة.

حظاً سعيداً !

By the end of this course you should be able to communicate with foreigners in English, either those people like British and Americans who speak English as a first language, or other nationalities such as Japanese, Filipinos, Swedes and Indians who have learned English as a second language. You should be able to read signs and write simple sentences.

Good luck!

UNIT 0 Check up!

Lesson 1 الدرس الأول

Look. أُنظر
Say. قل
Write. أُكتب
Listen. اِستمع
Read. اِقرأ
Match. (ضاهِ) ماثل
Ask. اِسأل
Answer. أجب

NUMBERS الأعداد

1 Look ١- أُنظر

0	1	2	3	4	5	6	7	8	9	10
٠	١	٢	٣	٤	٥	٦	٧	٨	٩	١٠

2 Match ٢- ماثل

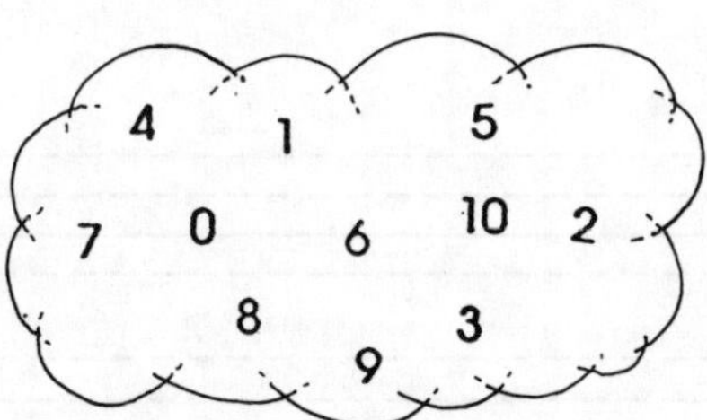

0 1 2 3 4 5 6 7 8 9 10

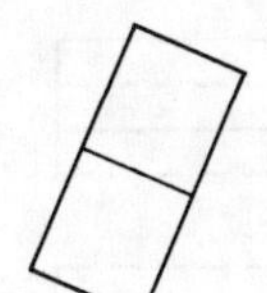  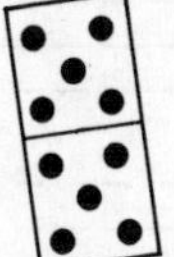   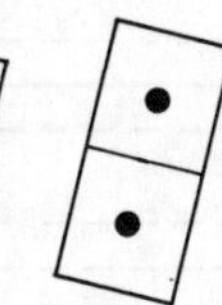 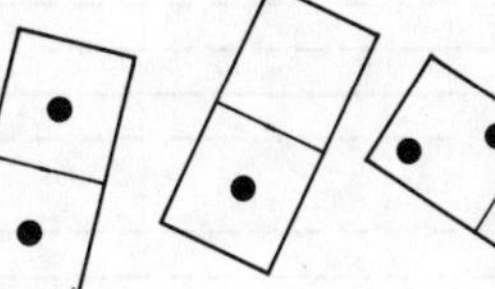 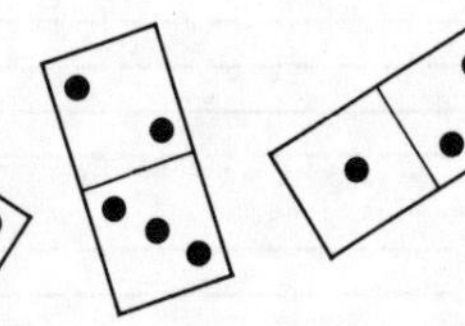 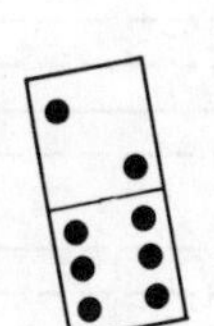 

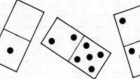

3 Listen ٣- اِستمع

0 1 2 3 4 5 6 7 8 9 10

4 Listen and draw ٤- إستمع وارسم

0 1 2 3 4 (5) 6 7 8 9 10

0 1 2 3 4 5 6 7 8 9 10

0 1 2 3 4 5 6 7 8 9 10

0 1 2 3 4 5 6 7 8 9 10

0 1 2 3 4 5 6 7 8 9 10

0 1 2 3 4 5 6 7 8 9 10

0 1 2 3 4 5 6 7 8 9 10

0 1 2 3 4 5 6 7 8 9 10

0 1 2 3 4 5 6 7 8 9 10

0 1 2 3 4 5 6 7 8 9 10

0 1 2 3 4 5 6 7 8 9 10

5 Write ٥- أكتب

Copy the numbers. إنسخ الأرقام

٦ 6 6 6

٧ 7 7 7

٨ 8 8 8

٩ 9 9 9

6 Write ٦- أكتب

Write the numbers. أُكتب الأعداد

3 ______ ______ ______ ______ ______

______ ______ ______ ______

7 Listen and write ٧- إستمع واكتب

Telephone numbers أرقام التليفونات

7 ______________ 3 ______________

8 ______________ 4 ______________

3 ______________ 0 ______________

Lesson 2/3 الدرس الثاني / الثالث

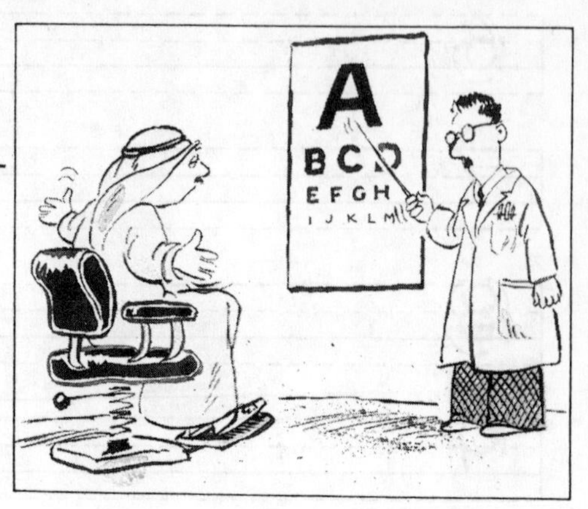

THE ALPHABET – Capital Letters حروف الهجاء – الحروف الكبيرة

A B C D E F G H I J K L M N O P Q R S T U V W X Y Z

1 Listen and say ١– إستمع وقل (كرر)

A H J K
B C D E G P T V
F L M N S X Z
I Y
O
Q U W
R

2 Read and match ٢– إقرأ وماثل

A	A	C	D	H	E	F	T	A	U	X	R	A
B	G	K	P	S	N	O	B	D	P	B	W	D
C	O	U	V	C	B	G	Q	C	T	U	C	G
D	B	D	E	Q	U	P	B	D	P	X	S	R
E	F	H	L	E	C	V	K	L	F	H	B	E
F	K	L	E	R	G	H	F	P	F	R	F	B
G	C	B	G	R	O	G	Q	C	G	H	Q	G
H	A	T	F	K	M	H	T	D	W	H	X	A
I	L	F	I	T	A	V	L	I	T	I	F	J
J	K	I	F	T	S	J	L	P	I	T	J	M
K	F	J	L	R	P	T	K	X	H	R	K	K
L	T	L	N	F	I	J	T	L	Z	V	T	L
M	N	V	M	L	W	M	V	N	M	W	D	H
N	B	G	I	N	W	P	Q	L	T	A	N	J
O	O	D	C	G	Q	O	D	Q	G	C	O	U
P	R	P	B	D	R	B	C	T	P	R	B	S
Q	U	G	Q	C	O	S	Q	G	O	Q	E	B
R	B	R	P	R	D	J	P	Y	R	S	P	B
S	F	B	H	M	Z	S	U	B	Z	G	S	H
T	H	F	E	L	I	F	T	B	T	E	I	T
U	V	U	Y	W	V	U	O	W	U	V	U	A

V	A	L	D	V	T	U	W	S	U	V	P	Q
W	U	H	X	K	W	V	B	V	L	W	U	A
X	X	H	D	S	W	X	V	Y	K	E	X	Y
Y	V	K	Y	S	T	Y	V	W	I	V	Y	X
Z	E	F	Z	X	F	S	T	K	V	A	Z	S

3 Read and say ٣- اِقرأ وقل

Read the abbreviations and match them with the pictures.

اِقرأ الاختصارات وضاهها (ماثلها) مع الصور

1) BBC
2) BMW
3) TV
4) FM
5) OK
6) KLM
7) MEA
8) UAE
9) UK
10) USA
11) BP
12) SOS

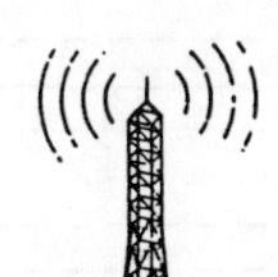

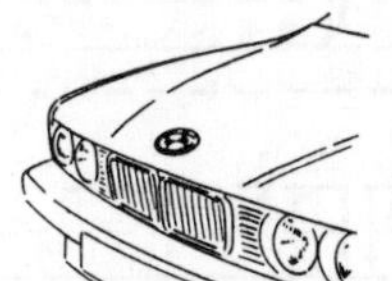

BBC ______ ______ ______ ______

______ ______ ______ ______

______ ______ ______ ______

Capital Letters الحروف الهجائية الكبيرة

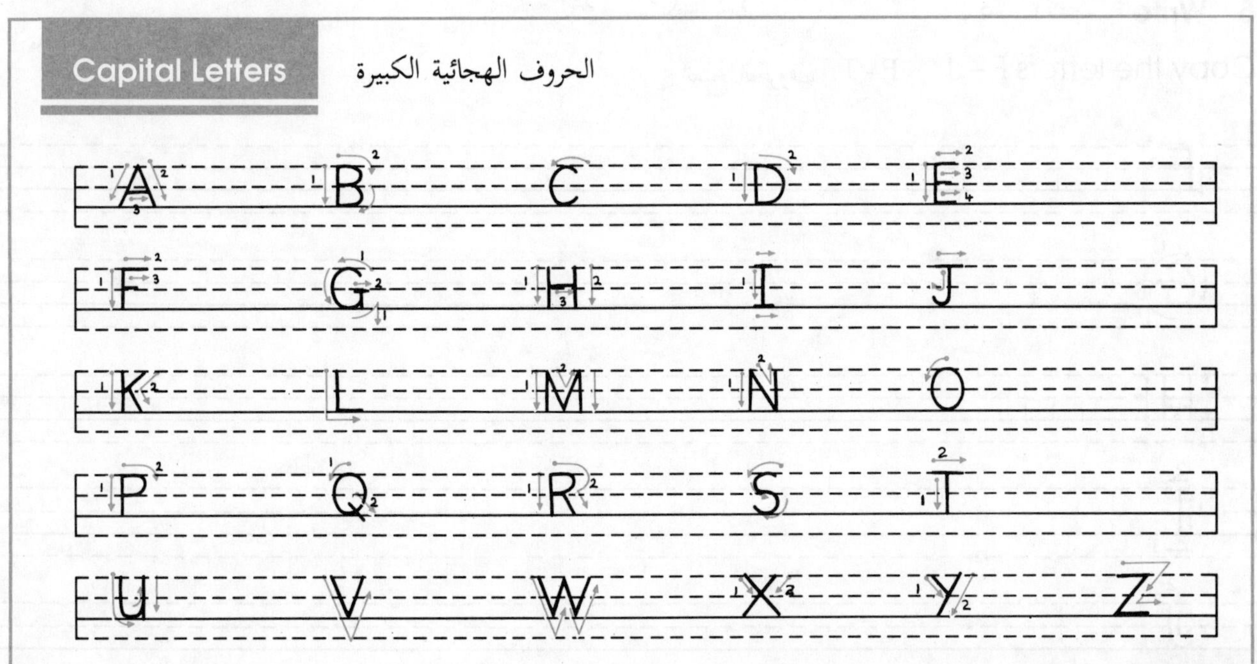

4 Write ٤- أُكتب

Copy the letters A – E. A - E إِنسخ الحروف

A A A

B B B

C C C

D D D

E E E

Now listen and write. والآن استمع واكتب

Bye–bye.

5 Write ٥- أُكتب

Copy the letters F – J. F - J إِنسخ الحروف

F F F

G G G

H H H

I I I

J J J

Now listen and write. والآن استمع واكتب

Hello. How are you?

Fine, thanks.

6 Write ٦- أُكتب

Copy the letters K – O. K - O اِنسخ الحروف

K K K

L L L

M M M

N N N

O O O

Now listen and write. والآن استمع واكتب

Are you Kuwaiti?

No, I'm Omani.

7 Write ٧- أُكتب

Copy the letters P – T. P - T اِنسخ الحروف

P

Q

R

S

T

Now listen and write. والآن استمع واكتب

Tea?

Thank you.

8 Write ٨- أُكتب

Copy the letters U – Z. U - Z اِنسخ الحروف

U

V

W

X

Y

Z

Now listen and write. والآن استمع واكتب

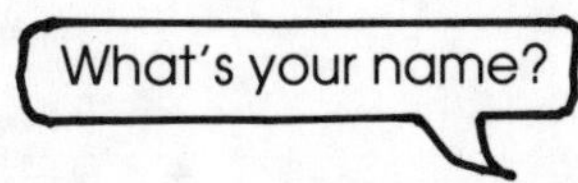

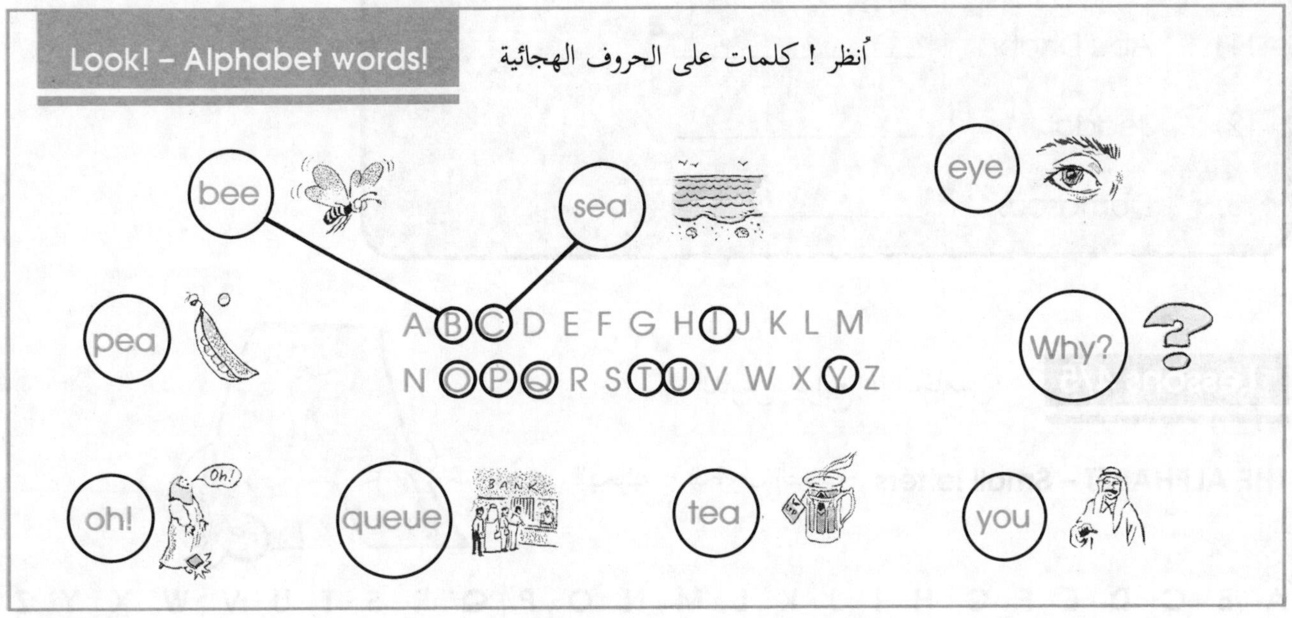

9 Listen اِستمع

Passport numbers أرقام جواز السفر

1) 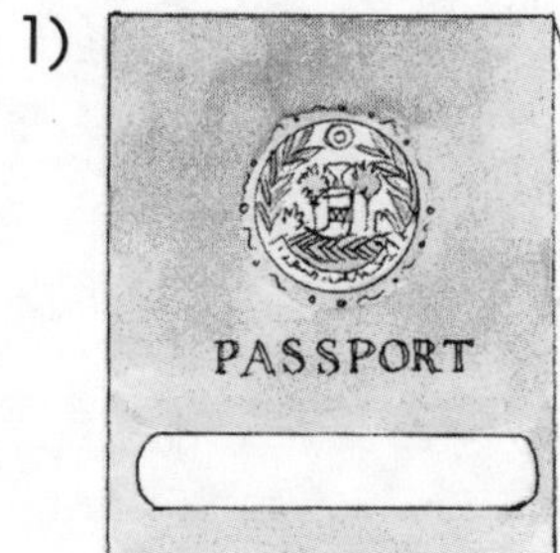

2) 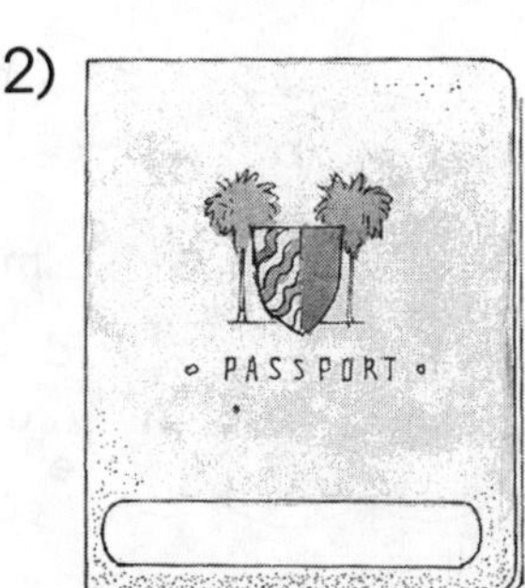

3) 

4) 

Car numbers أرقام السيارات

5) 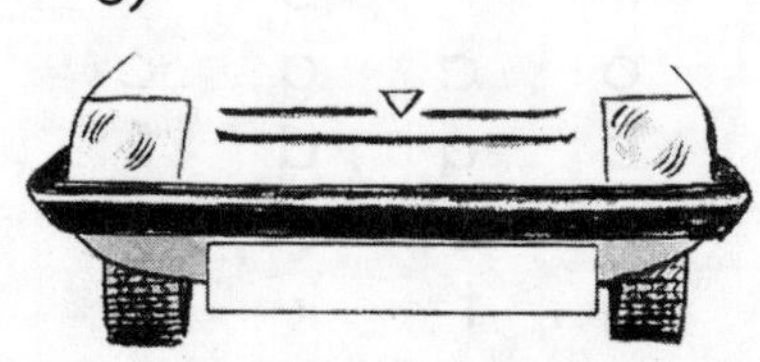

6) 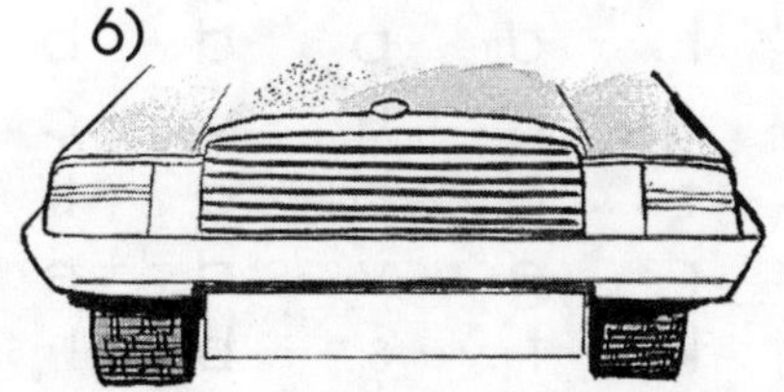

7) 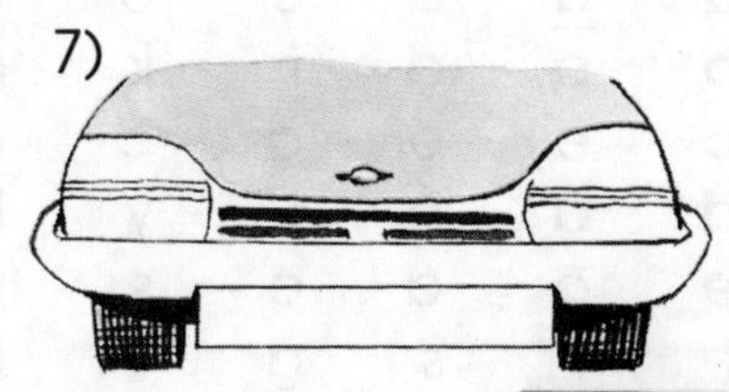

Flight numbers أرقام الرحلات الجوية

		Flight number
8)	Cairo	________
9)	London	________
10)	Tunis	________
11)	Abu Dhabi	________
12)	Jeddah	________
13)	Damascus	________

Lessons 4/5 الدرس الرابع / الخامس

THE ALPHABET – Small letters الحروف الهجائية – الحروف الصغيرة

A	B	C	D	E	F	G	H	I	J	K	L	M	N	O	P	Q	R	S	T	U	V	W	X	Y	Z
a	b	c	d	e	f	g	h	i	j	k	l	m	n	o	p	q	r	s	t	u	v	w	x	y	z

1 Match ١– ماثل

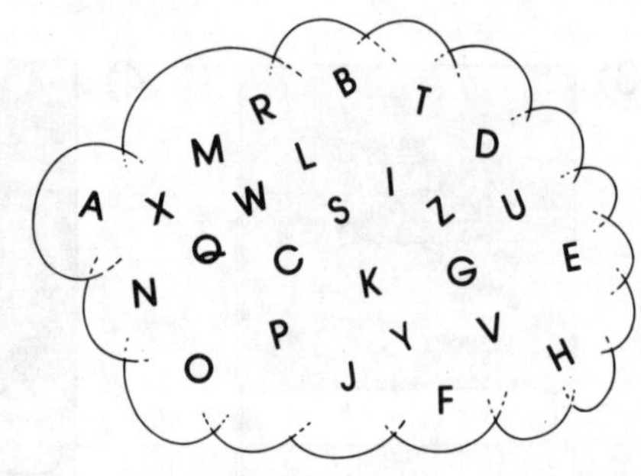

2 Match ٢– ماثل

a	<u>a</u>	c	e	o	e	u	v	e	<u>a</u>	s	c	o	<u>a</u>	e	x
b	p	d	f	k	b	l	d	p	d	b	l	k	t	b	d
c	e	o	d	c	e	q	o	u	v	c	d	o	a	g	c
d	d	b	t	y	k	t	d	b	d	t	p	b	q	d	f
e	o	a	c	s	u	r	e	v	d	e	a	o	e	s	g
f	t	s	g	f	h	k	t	s	b	l	f	g	t	k	d

g	g	p	q	h	g	j	y	q	p	d	g	q	d	p	j
h	m	k	f	t	n	b	h	k	t	f	h	d	l	h	n
i	i	l	j	t	v	i	y	l	j	t	j	i	y	f	l
j	y	l	g	i	q	p	j	l	i	j	y	q	f	p	i
k	h	f	b	k	h	x	t	j	c	f	d	x	v	h	t
l	t	f	i	k	f	l	t	f	b	i	l	d	j	t	h
m	m	u	w	n	v	r	x	m	w	g	e	m	n	o	m
n	r	h	k	m	o	n	u	v	n	r	u	s	n	u	m
o	u	o	n	q	a	d	o	p	u	x	d	v	u	o	r
p	q	b	p	h	q	b	h	p	g	p	d	h	b	g	p
q	p	d	g	q	j	g	y	d	q	g	d	j	p	g	y
r	r	n	m	o	v	u	n	r	o	u	r	m	v	t	r
s	x	a	z	v	s	e	z	a	e	x	v	y	x	e	s
t	h	d	f	j	t	l	h	t	f	j	k	l	t	i	f
u	n	u	v	m	r	y	u	v	n	m	y	o	u	v	n
v	r	e	y	x	u	y	n	v	r	v	u	y	r	m	x
w	u	m	n	v	u	w	x	v	w	m	n	a	w	v	u
x	x	z	s	k	v	h	x	u	k	z	r	s	f	h	x
y	p	g	j	u	y	q	j	y	j	p	q	v	y	u	g
z	s	e	z	a	x	a	v	k	z	s	k	x	v	s	e

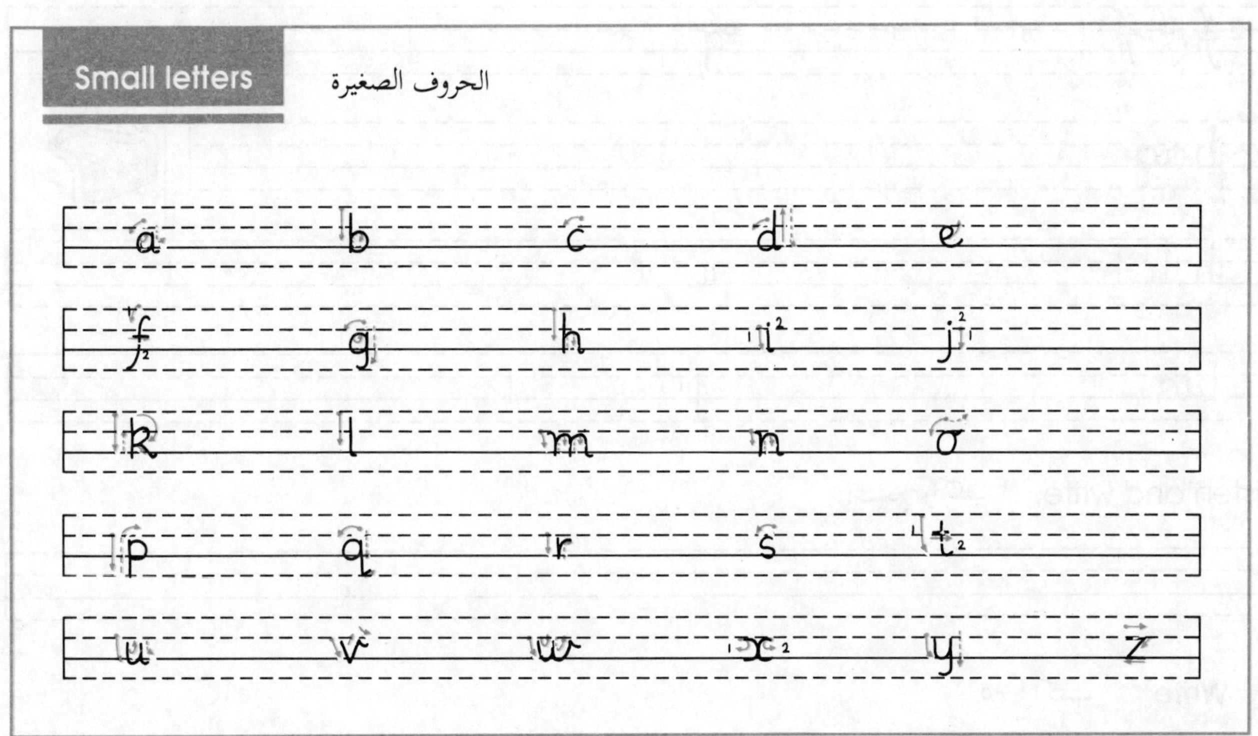

3 Write ٣- أُكتب

Copy the letters a – e. إنسخ الحروف a - e

a a a

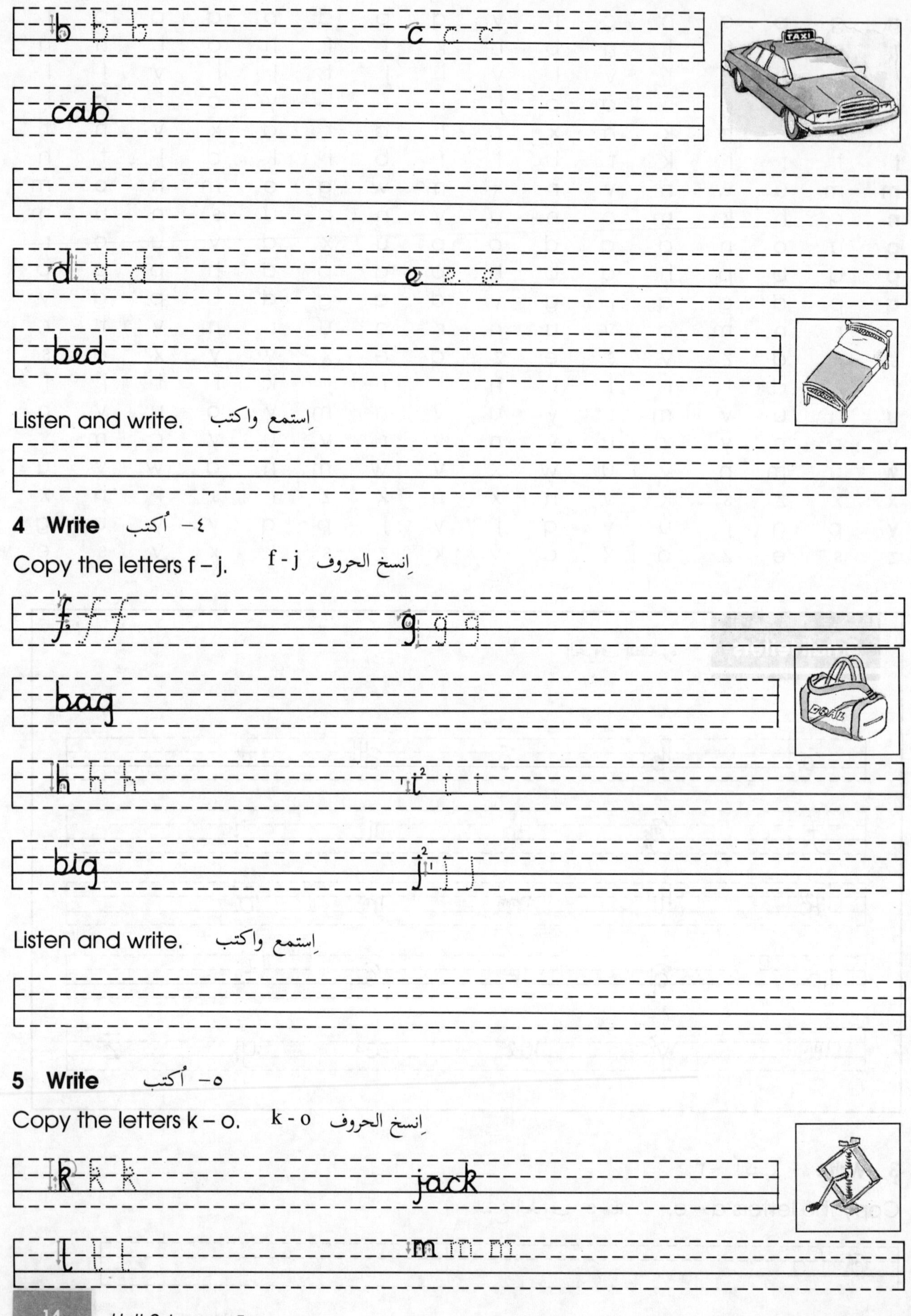

Listen and write. اِستمع واكتب

4 Write ٤- اُكتب

Copy the letters f – j. f - j اِنسخ الحروف

Listen and write. اِستمع واكتب

5 Write ٥- اُكتب

Copy the letters k – o. k - o اِنسخ الحروف

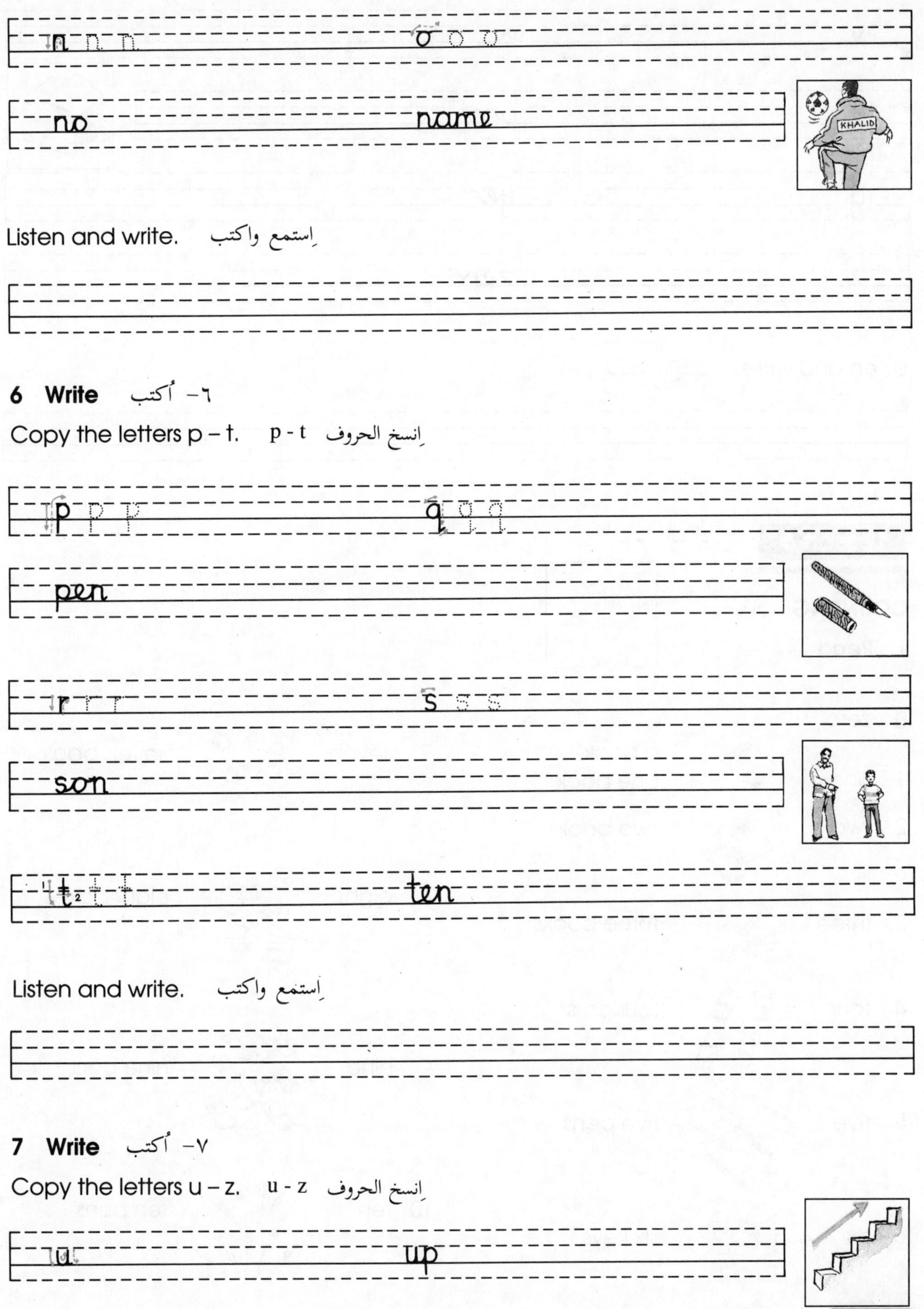

Listen and write. اِستمع واكتب

6 Write ٦- أُكتب

Copy the letters p – t. p - t اِنسخ الحروف

Listen and write. اِستمع واكتب

7 Write ٧- أُكتب

Copy the letters u – z. u - z اِنسخ الحروف

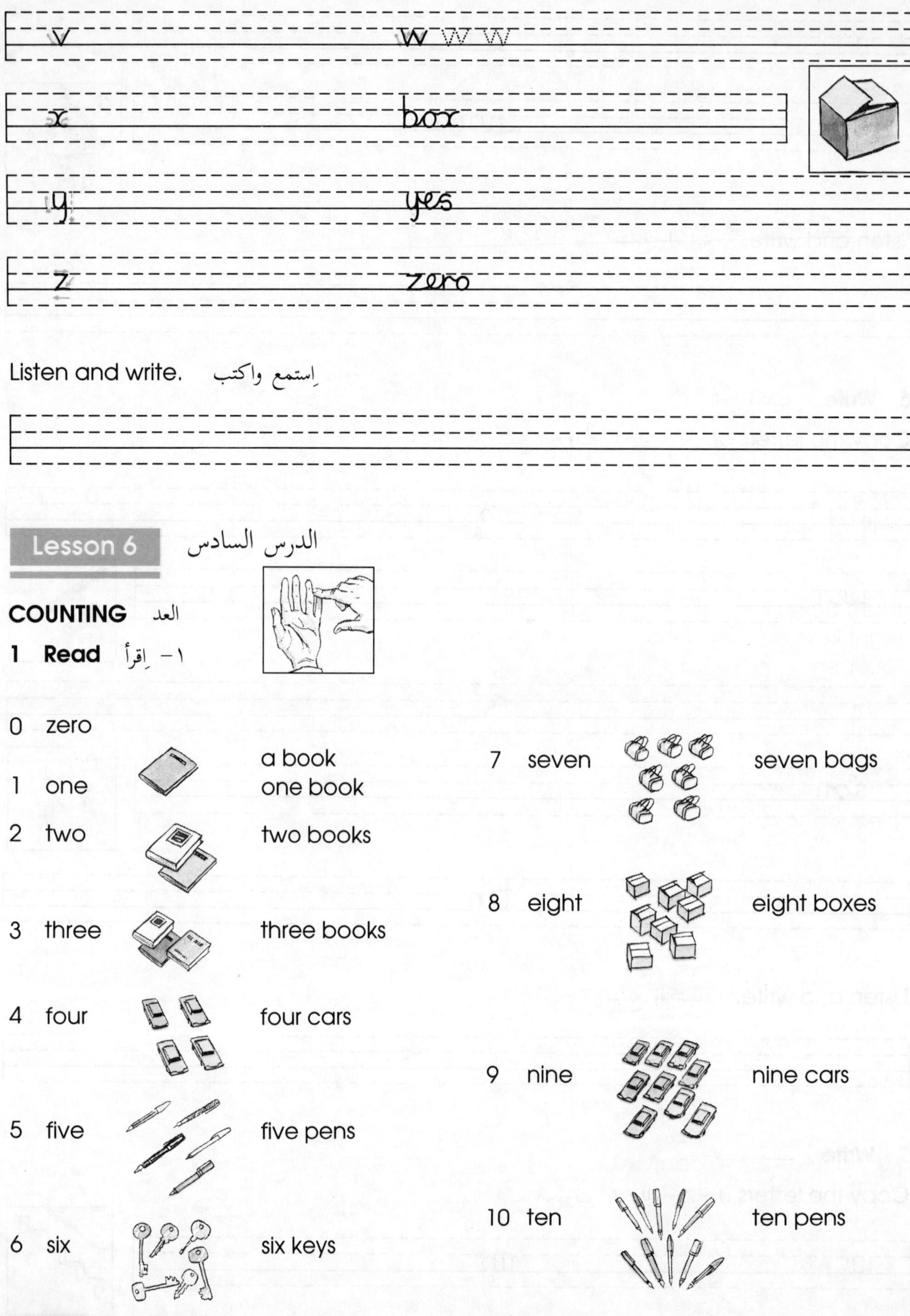

Listen and write. اِستمع واكتب

Lesson 6 الدرس السادس

COUNTING العد

1 Read ١ – اِقرأ

0 zero

1 one — a book / one book

2 two — two books

3 three — three books

4 four — four cars

5 five — five pens

6 six — six keys

7 seven — seven bags

8 eight — eight boxes

9 nine — nine cars

10 ten — ten pens

2 Listen and draw ٢- إستمع وارسم

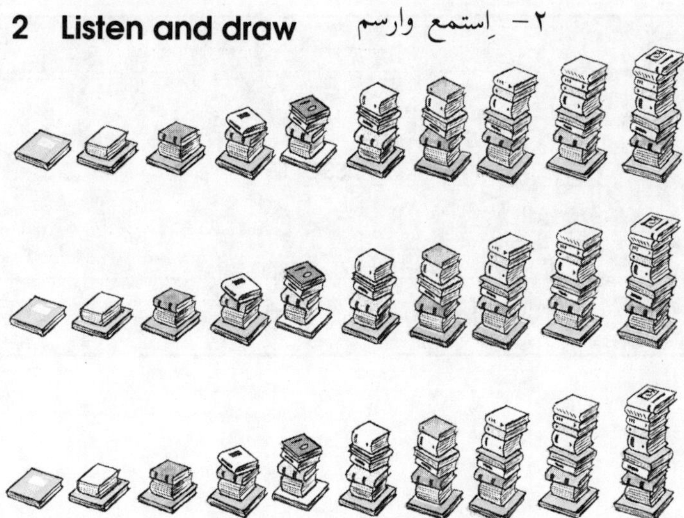

3 Read and match ٣- إقرأ وماثل

six books
two bags
four cars
a mosque
three boxes
eight keys
four pens
one man
two bees

a)

b)

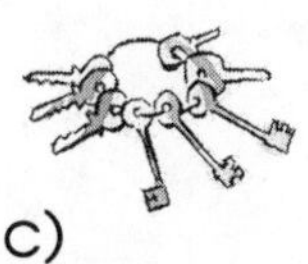
c)

d)

e)

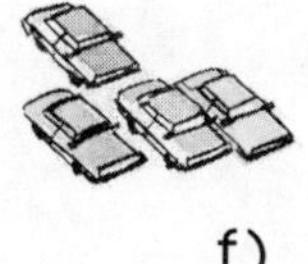
f)

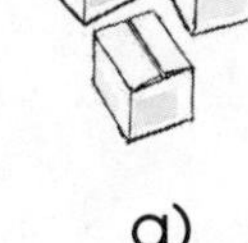
g)

h)

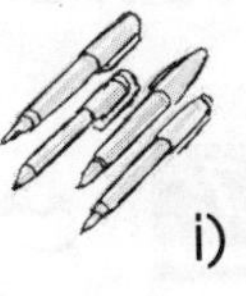
i)

NAMES الأسماء

1 Read ١- إقرأ

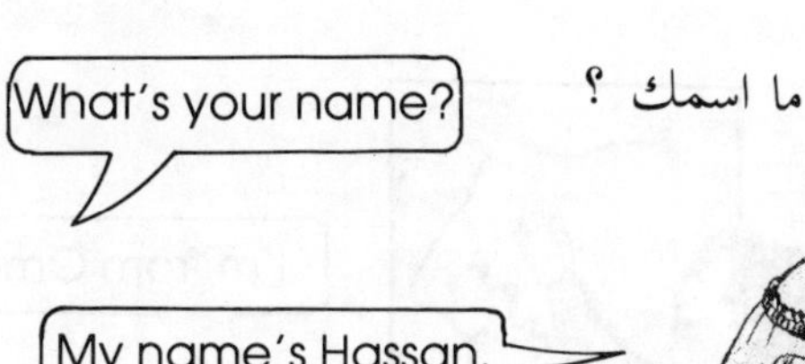
What's your name?

ما اسمك ؟

My name's Hassan.

My name's Latifa.

My name's	Mohammad	My name's	Selwa
	Ali		Nora
	Tawfiq		Jamila
	Waleed		Mariam
	Khalid		Samira
	Yasser		Khadija

Look! أُنظر ! الحرف الأول حرف كبير

The first letter is a capital letter.

Hassan

capital letter — small letters

2 Write ٢– أُكتب

What's your name?

My name's Mohammad Yousef.

What's your name?

My name's

Lesson 7 الدرس السابع

COUNTRIES البلاد

1 Read ١– اِقرأ

Where are you from?

EGYPT
I'm from Egypt.

OMAN
I'm from Oman.

Look! أُنظر ! الحرف الأول حرف كبير

The first letter is a capital letter.

Oman

capital letter — small letters

2 Write ٢- أُكتب

I'm from Egypt. Where are you from?

Qatar			Libya
Morocco		Bahrain	
	Sudan		Oman
Algeria		Egypt	Tunisia
	Iraq		Yemen
United Arab Emirates (UAE)		Syria	Jordan
	Saudi Arabia	Lebanon	
Kuwait			Palestine

I'm from ______

CITIES المدن

1 Read ١- إقرأ

Where are you from?
I'm from Cairo.

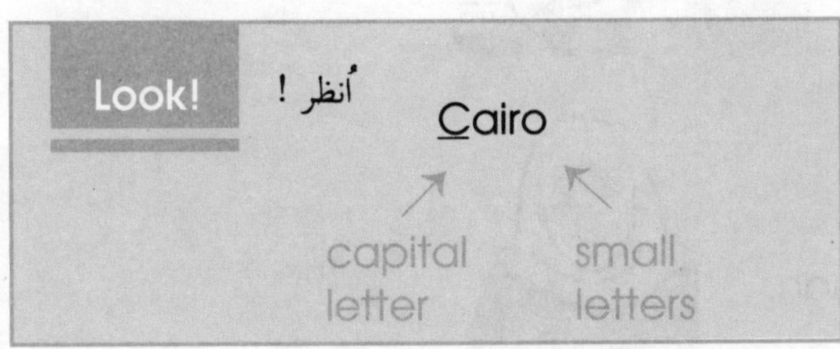
Look! أُنظر !
Cairo
capital letter
small letters

2 Write ٢- أكتب

Where are you from? I'm from ____________________

3 Match ٣- ماثل

City **Country**

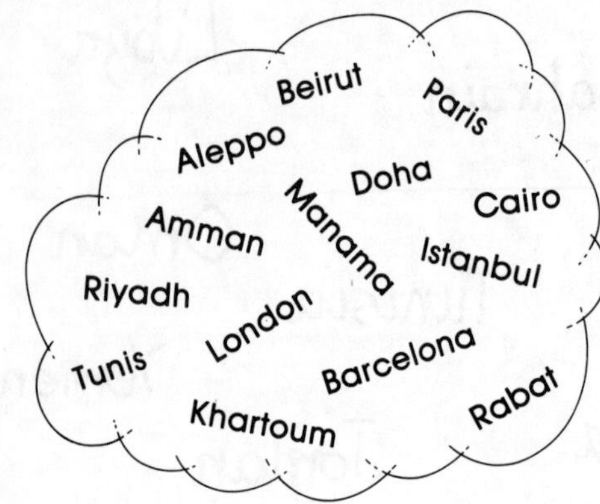

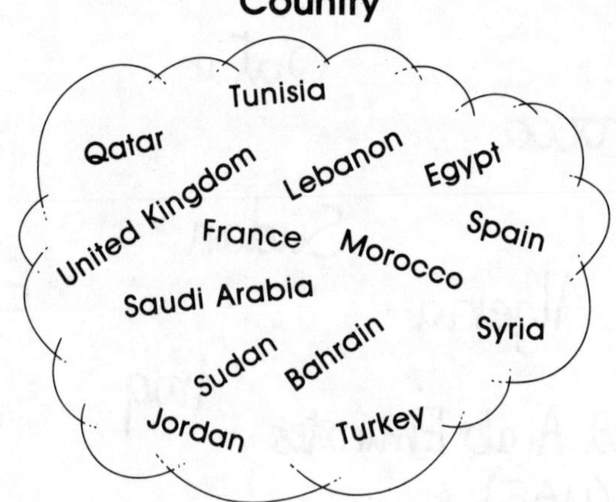

4 Write ٤- أكتب

Name: ____________________

City: ____________________

Country: ____________________

Telephone number: ____________________

Lesson 8 الدرس الثامن

PUNCTUATION علامات الترقيم

full stop	.	النقطة – علامة الوقف	question mark	?	مة الاستفهام
comma	,	الفاصلة	apostrophe	'	صلة العليا
exclamation mark	!	علامة التعجب			

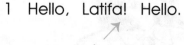

1 Hello, Latifa! Hello.

exclamation mark

2 How are you? Fine, thar

question mark comma

apostrophe

3 My name's Latifa. I'm from Oman.

WORDS الكلمات

Read اِقرأ

Here are 24 English words you already know! Write in the Arabic.

هنا ٢٦ كلمة إنجليزية تعرفها من قبل اُكتبها باللغة العربية

A a
aspirin ____________________

B b
battery ____________________

C c
camera ____________________

D d
dozen ____________________

E e
express ____________________

F f
film ____________________

G g
goal ____________________

H h
Happy Birthday ______________

I i
ice-cream ____________________

J j
jacket ____________________

K k
karate ____________________

L l
lemonade ____________________

M m
mechanic ____________________

N n
nurse ____________________

O o
offside ____________________

P p
passport ____________________

R r
radio ____________________

S s
sandwich ____________________

T t
taxi ____________________

V v
video ____________________

W w
workshop ____________________

X x
X-ray ____________________

Y y
yacht ____________________

Z z
zebra ____________________

UNIT 1 Meeting People

Lesson 1 Hello! الدرس الأول : مرحبا

1 Listen and write ١- اِستمع واكتب

Write A, B, C or D.

2 Ask and answer ٢- اِسأل وأجب

Practise with other students in the class.

Hello. I'm … **Hello …, I'm …**
How are you? **Fine, thanks.**

3 Names ٣- الأسماء

Mary Brown — Hello, Mary
Hello, Mrs Brown

Tom Brown — Hello, Tom
Hello, Mr Brown

Mark James — Hello …
Hello …

Sue Long — Hello …
....

John Main — Hello …
....

4 Say ٤- قل

Choose a name. Practise with a partner.

Hello, I'm … **Hello Mr/Mrs …, I'm …**

Look! أُنظر !

I'm Tom Brown.
I am Tom Brown.

5 Listen and write ٥- اِستمع واكتب

Write A, B, C or D.

Write under each picture: **Hello? Hello! Hello? Hello.**

Language اللغة

Hello/Hi.	Mr …
I'm …	Mrs …
I am …	
How are you?	Fine thanks.

Lesson 2 My name's Bond

الدرس الثاني : اسمي بوند

1 Listen and write ١- اِستمع واكتب

Write A, B, C or D.

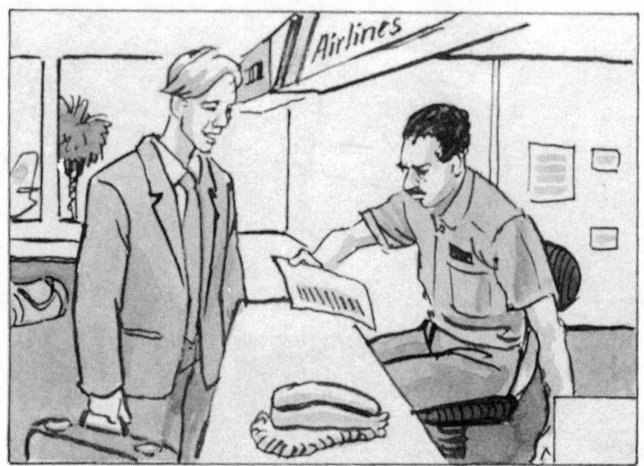

What's your name, please?
Main, John Main.
M - A - N - E?
No. M - A - I - N.

Hello. Are you Mrs Brown?
Yes.
My name's Nadia.
Oh, hello, Nadia. How are you?

Hello, Mr Darwish?
No. My name's Mohammad Yousef.
Oh, I'm sorry.

That's all right.

Hello. My name's Tom Brown.
Hello, Mr Brown. How are you?
I'm fine, thank you.

2 Ask and answer ٢- اِسأل وأجب

Practise with other students in the class.

Hello. My name's ...
Hello, ... How are you?
I'm fine, thank you.

3 Listen and say ٣- اِستمع وقل

sorry

thank you

How are you?

hello

all right

4 Ask and answer ٤- اِسأل وأجب

I'm sorry.
That's all right.

Practise with other students.

Hello. Mr Darwish? **No. My name's ...**
Oh, I'm sorry. **That's all right.**

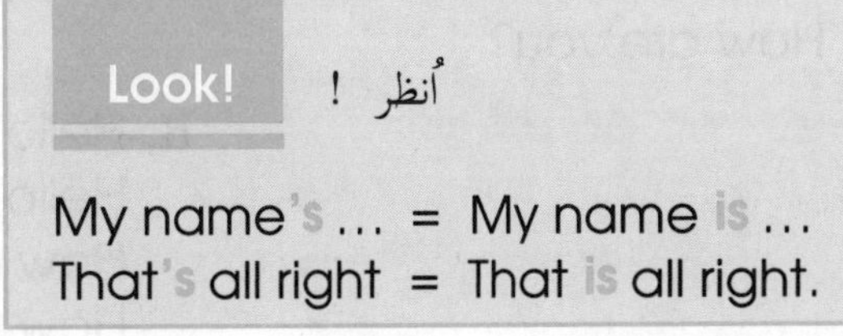

Look! ! أُنظر

My name's ... = My name is ...
That's all right = That is all right.

5 Read and say ٥- اِقرأ وقل

Spell these names. For example:

Main - M - A - I - N.

Kent, Brown, Sarah, Ward, Darwish, Jones, Rashid, Yousef, Clark, Latifa, Barry, Smith.

Language اللغة

Are you ...?
What's your name, please?

My name's ...
I'm fine.
I'm sorry.
That's all right.
Thank you.

Lesson 3 **This is Ahmed** الدرس الثالث : هذا هو أحمد

1 Listen and write ١- اِستمع واكتب

Write A, B, or C.

A Ali, this is my friend Tom.
Hello, Ali.
Hi. How are you?

B Hello, Selwa. How are you?
Hello, Mary. I'm fine, thanks. Mary, this is Fatima.
How do you do?
How do you do?

C Hello, Ahmed. How are you?
Oh, not bad, thanks. Sam, this is Saleem Saeedi.
How do you do, Mr Saeedi?
Pleased to meet you.

2 Listen and say ٢- اِستمع وقل

How do you do?

Pleased to meet you.

3 Ask and answer ٣- اِسأل وأجب

Introduce other students like this:

A: **Hello, ... This is ....**
B: **How do you do?**
C: **How do you do? / Pleased to meet you.**

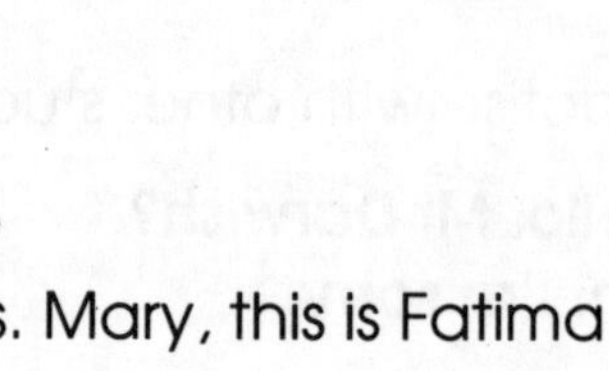

4 Listen and say ٤- اِستمع وقل

Numbers 0–5: 0 – **zero** 1 – **one** 2 – **two** 3 – **three** 4 – **four** 5 – **five.**

5 Listen and say ٥- اِستمع وقل

The alphabet:

A B C D E F G H I J K L M N O P Q R S T U V W X Y Z

Listen and say these letters.

A, H, J, K
B, C, D, E, G, P, T, V
F, L, M, N, S, X, Z

I, Y
O
Q, U, W
R

6 Read and say ٦- اِقرأ وقل

Read these car numbers to a partner.

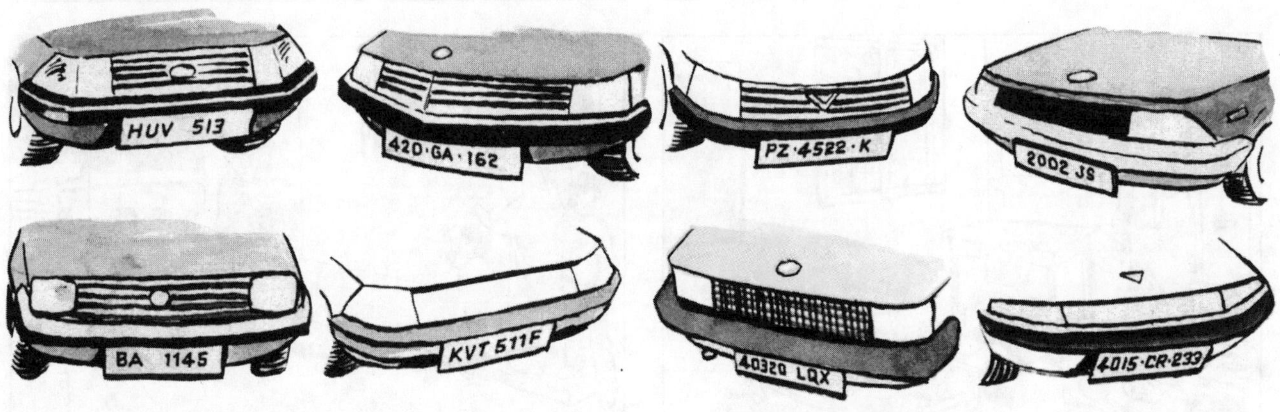

Look! أنظر !

is

My name is Tom. (My name's Tom.)
That is all right. (That's all right.)
This is Ahmed.

Language اللغة

This is ...
Pleased to meet you.
Not bad.

friend
first name
family name
numbers: 0–5

Lesson 4 Good morning صباح الخير : الدرس الرابع

Good morning.

1 Listen and write ١- اِستمع واكتب

Write A, B, C or D.

A Good night.
Good night.

B Good afternoon, ITC.
Hello. My name's John Main.

C Good morning.
Good morning.

D Good evening.
Good evening, Mr Main.
How are you?
Fine thanks. And you?
I'm fine.

2 Listen and say ٢- اِستمع وقل

morning afternoon night

evening

3 Write ٣- أُكتب

Write **afternoon, evening, morning, night** below the picture.

4 Ask and answer ٤- إسأل وأجب

Use: morning/afternoon/evening; fine/not bad/I'm fine, thank you, to greet other students like this:

5 Listen and say ٥- إستمع وقل

Numbers 6–10:

6 – **six** 7 – **seven** 8 – **eight** 9 – **nine** 10 – **ten**.

6 Read ٦- إقرأ

Read these signs:

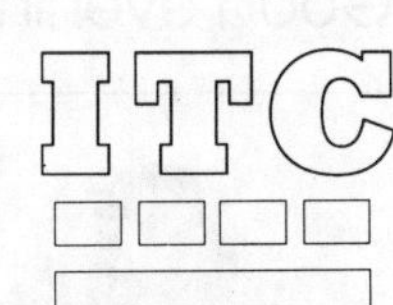
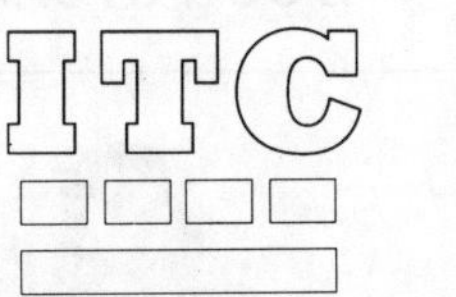

Now read these telephone numbers:

837–987, 246–193, 504–451, 632–018, 792–650, 437–915.

Language اللغة

Good morning afternoon evening night	And you? telephone number

STUDY أُدرس

Hello/Hi.
I'm …
My name's …
What's your name, please?

This is Ahmed.

How are you?

Fine thanks.
I'm fine, thank you.
Not bad.

I'm sorry.

That's all right.

How do you do?

How do you do?
Pleased to meet you.

Are you …?

Yes.
No.

Good morning

Good afternoon

Good evening

Good night

Mr … 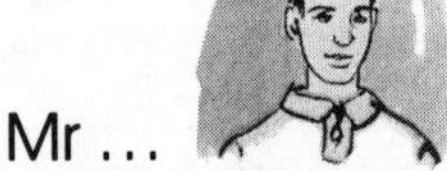

Mrs … 

am

I'm fine.
I'm Tom Brown.
I'm sorry.

I am fine.
I am Tom Brown.
I am sorry.

are

Are you Mrs Brown?
How **are** you?

is

What's your name?
My name's Mohammad Yousef.
That's all right.
This **is** my friend.

What **is** your name?
My name **is** Mohammad Yousef.
That **is** all right.

NEW WORDS كلمات جديدة

Learn these words. تعلم هذه الكلمات

yes
no
a name
a friend
morning
afternoon
evening
night
first
a family
a number
a telephone
a flight
a passport

numbers 0–10

zero, one, two, three, four, five, six, seven, eight, nine, ten.

Write other new words here. أكتب الكلمات الجديدة الأخرى

UNIT 2 Family and Friends

Lesson 1 Who's that?

 **1 Listen**

Who's that?
That's my grandfather, Ali.
He's handsome.

And this is my sister.
She's nice, What's her name?
Mariam.

Is this your son?
Yes. His name's Ahmed.

And who's this? She's nice too.
Oh, thank you. That's me!

Write the names.  

grandfather – ________ sister – ________ son – ________

2 Write

This is Latifa's family. Write in: **husband, son, daughter**.

Now write in: **sister, brother, mother, father, grandmother, uncle, grandfather.**

Look!

my, your, his, her

My, name's Latifa.
What's **your** name?

This is my sister. What's **her** name?
This is my son. What's **his** name?

3 Write

Write **his** or **her**.

a) This is my daughter.
   What's ________ name?
b) This is my father. ________ name's Mohammad.
c) This is my brother.
   What's ________ name?
d) This is my grandmother. ________ name's Nora.
e) This is my husband. ________ name's Abdul Karim.
f) And that's my uncle.
   What's ________ name?

4 Listen and say

These words end in **-er**.

a) daught**er**, fath**er**, teach**er**, sist**er**

These words all have the letters **th**.

b) **th**is **th**at mo**th**er bro**th**er

c) **th**anks **th**ree

Look!

A: That's my grandfather.
B: **He's** handsome.
A: This is my sister, Mariam.
B: **She's** nice.

5 Ask and answer

Look at Latifa's photos. Ask and answer with another student.

Who's that? **That's her grandfather.**

Now ask and answer with these pictures.

Who's that/this? **That's her ...**
I don't know.

Language

Who's that?	Who's this?	I don't know.
This is ...		
That is ...		
What's **her** name?	**Her** name's ...	**She's** nice.
What's **his** name?	**His** name's ...	**He's** handsome. too

Lesson 2 Good Luck Hotel

1 Read

How do you do? I'm Hassan. This is my hotel.
It's very good and it's cheap.
Good Luck HOTEL

This is my son. His name's Mohsin.
He's eight years old.
Yes, I'm eight.
And this is my daughter. Her name's Jamila. She's very young.
How old are you, Jamila?
I'm five and a half.

Write the answers.

a) How old is Mohsin? He's ________________ years old.

b) How old is Jamila? She's ________________ years old.

2 Write

Write **she's, he's** or **it's**.

a) 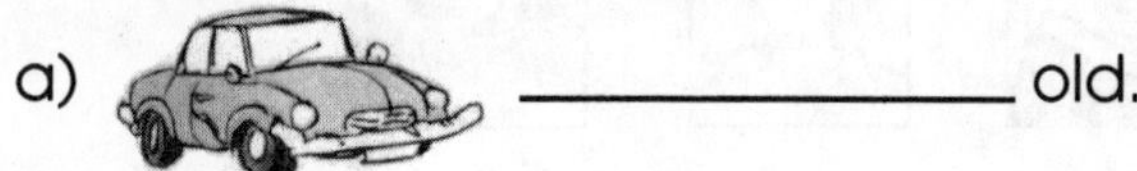 ________________ old.

b) 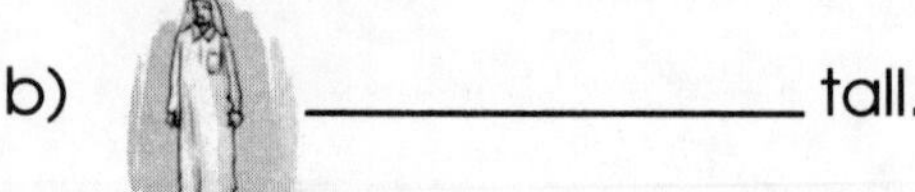 ________________ tall.

c) 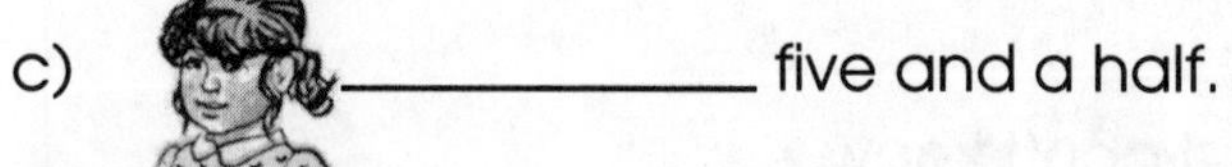 ________________ five and a half.

d) 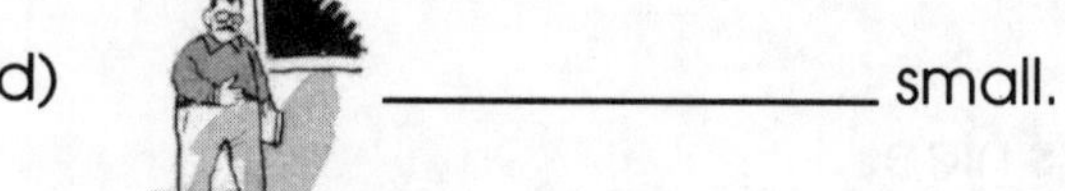 ________________ small.

e)  ________________ new.

This is my daughter. **She's** five and a half.
This is my son. **He's** eight.
This is my hotel. **It's** good. **It's** cheap.

f)  ________________ big.

g)  ________________ nice.

3 Match

Match the adjectives with opposite meanings.

good
expensive
new
short
young
cheap
small
tall
old
big
old
bad

4 Ask and answer

Is it …? **No. It's …**
Is he …?
Is she …?

Example: Is it old? No. It's new.

Look!

Questions

It is new. (It's new.)	**Is it** new?
He is seven. (He's seven.)	How old **is he**?
She is young.	**Is she** young?

a) young? 

b) tall? 

c) good? 

d) big? 

e) new? 

f) cheap? 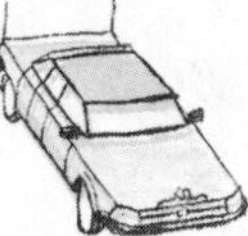

5 Listen and say

telephone grandfather expensive afternoon

6 Listen and say

Numbers 11–15:

11 – **eleven** 12 – **twelve** 13 – **thirteen** 14 – **fourteen** 15 – **fifteen**

$\frac{1}{2}$ – **a half** 5$\frac{1}{2}$ – **five and a half** 12$\frac{1}{2}$ – **twelve and a half**

Language

I'm ...	I am
You're ...	You are
He's ...	He is
She's ...	She is
It's ...	It is

Is he ...?
Is she ...?
Is it ...?

How old is she?
is he?
are you?

She is ... years old.

Lesson 3 Where are you from?

1 Match

Match these countries with the maps: Oman, Egypt, England, America (USA).

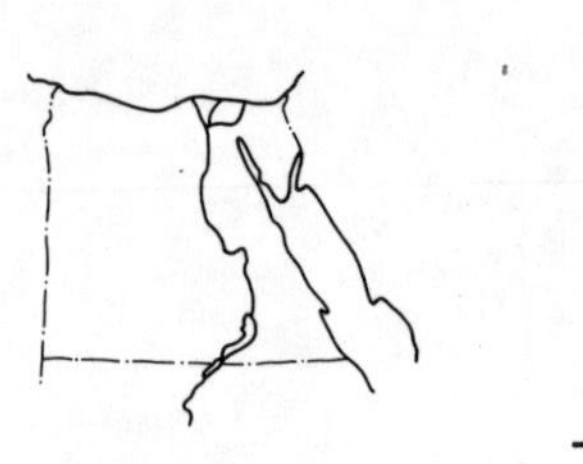

2 Listen

Write in the name of the country.

A

Where are you from, Hassan?

I'm from Tanta.

Where's that?

It's in ___________.

B

What's your name please?

Brown, Mary Brown.

And where are you from, Mrs Brown?

I'm from ___________.

C

Are you from ___________, Sam?

Yes, I am. I'm from the ___________.

From New York?

New York? No! I'm from Dallas. That's in Texas.

D

Are you from Kuwait, Latifa?

No, I'm not. I'm from Sur.

Sur? Where's that?

It's in ___________.

3 Listen and say

Where are you from? I'm from England.

4 Ask and answer

Choose a city and a country from the list. Ask three students:

Where are you from?	**I'm from …**	Oran/Algeria
Where's that?	**It's in …**	Sousse/Tunisia
		Al Hufuf/Saudi Arabia
		Latakia/Syria

5 Ask and answer

Practise with another student.

Where's Hassan from?	**He's from …**
Mary	**She's from …**
Sam	
Latifa	

Look!

I am	from Oman.	(I'm …)
You are	from England.	(You're …)
He is	from Egypt.	(He's …)
She is	from Oman.	(She's …)
It is	in Oman.	(It's …)

6 Write

Write **am, are**, or **is** in the spaces.

A: Where ____________ you from?

B: I ____________ from Latakia.

A: Where ____________ that?

B: It ____________ in Syria.

A: And where ____________ your friend from?

B: She ____________ from Aleppo. That ____________ in Syria, too.

IMMIGRATION
Where are you from?

Language

Where are you from?	I'm from …
Where's that?	It's in …
Are you from …?	
Where's … from?	He's from …
	She's from …

Lesson 4 **Welcome!**

1 Listen

Officer: What's your name please?
Tom: Tom Brown.
Officer: How do you spell that?
Tom: B-R-O-W-N, Brown.
Officer: Where are you from?
Tom: I'm from England.
Officer: Are you from London?
Tom: No, I'm not. I'm from Manchester.
Officer: Welcome to Jordan, Mr Brown.

2 Write

Complete the immigration form.

Immigration form

NAME: ______________________

CITY: ______________________

COUNTRY: ______________________

PASSPORT NO. FH 29431706

3 Read

Match the sign with the picture.

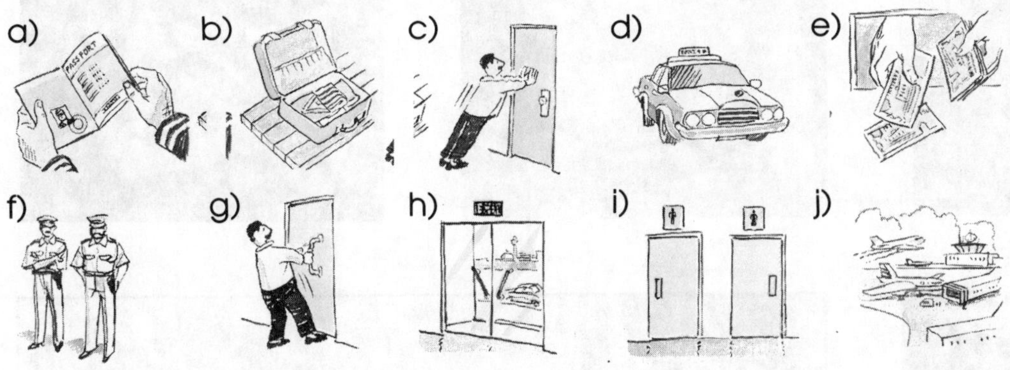

4 Listen and say

Numbers 16–20:

16 – **sixteen** 17 – **seventeen** 18 – **eighteen** 19 – **nineteen** 20 – **twenty**.

5 Listen and say

These words all have the **p** sound:

push, pull, please, spell, passport,

Pepsi, expensive, police.

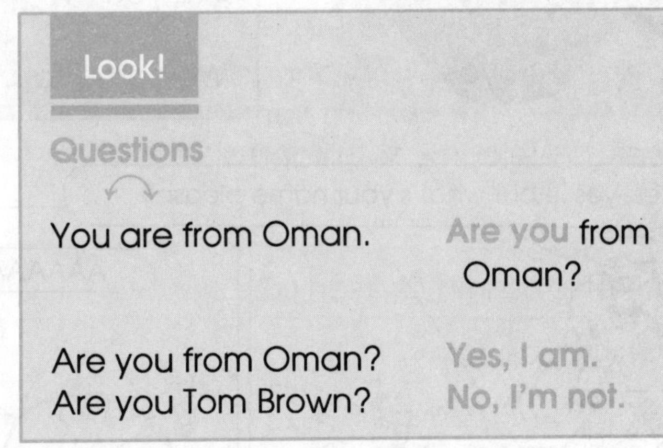

Look!

Questions

You are from Oman.	Are you from Oman?
Are you from Oman?	Yes, I am.
Are you Tom Brown?	No, I'm not.

6 A game

Who are you?

Are you from ...? **Yes, I am.**

Are you ...? **No, I'm not.**

Choose one of the people on the next page.

Language

How do you spell ...?

Are you from ...?	Yes, I am.
Are you ...?	No, I'm not.

Welcome to ...

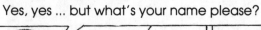

Yes, yes ... but what's your name please?

AAAAAAHH!

How do you spell that?

STUDY

I am …	(I'm)
You are …	(You're)
He is …	(He's)
She is …	(She's)
It is …	(It's)

I'm	eighteen.
You're	from Cairo.
He's	handsome.
She's	very young.
It's	in Yemen.

Are you Mrs Brown? — Yes, I am.
Are you from London? — No, I'm not.

Is he very young?  He's old.

Is she tall?  She's short.

Is it new? It's old.

Who Who's this?  Who's that? 

What What's your name?

Where Where are you from?
Where's that?

How

How are you?	Fine thanks.
How do you do?	Pleased to meet you.
How do you spell that?	B-R-O-W-N
How old are you?	I'm 29.

my, your, his, her

My name's Bond, James Bond.
What's **your** telephone number?
This is Hassan and this is **his** son.
Her name's Habiba. She's from Taif.

too

Hassan's from Sharjah. Fatima's from Sharjah **too**.

NEW WORDS

Learn these words.

family

mother
father
sister
brother
grandfather
son
daughter
wife
husband
aunt
uncle
cousin

countries

Algeria
Egypt
England
Jordan
Kuwait
Oman
Tunisia
Saudi Arabia
Syria
The United States of America (USA)

adjectives

big
small
tall
short
good
bad
nice
handsome
young
old
new
cheap
expensive

numbers 11–20

eleven, twelve, thirteen, fourteen, fifteen, sixteen, seventeen, eighteen, nineteen, twenty.

a half

Review Unit A

Grammar

1 Write

I am …	(I'm)
You are …	(You're)
He is …	(He's)
She is …	(She's)
It is …	(It's)

Write **I, you, he, she** or **it** in the spaces.

a) Hello, _____'m Mohammad Yousef.

b) How are ______?

c) _____'m fine thanks.

d) Are _____ Latifa Al-Rashid?

e) No, _____'m not.

f) Oh, _____'m sorry.

This is my car.

g) Is _____ new?

h) No. _____'s old.

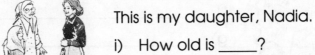

This is my daughter, Nadia.

i) How old is _____?

j) _____'s twelve.

This is my friend, Abed.

k) Where's _____ from?

l) _____'s from Doha.

Where's that?

m) _____'s in Qatar.

2 Write

Questions

I am …	Am I …?	*Question words*
You are …	Are you …?	**What …?** **How …?** **How old …?**
He is …	Is he …?	
She is …	Is she …?	**Where …?** **Who …?**
It is …	Is it …?	
This is …	Is this …?	

Are you from London?
Is he young?
Is this your son?

Write the questions.

a) ______________________? My name's Clare Smith.

b) ______________________? C-L-A-R-E S-M-I-T-H

c) ______________________? I'm 19.

d) ______________________? From America.

e) ______________________? No, I'm not from New York. I'm from Dallas.

f) ______________________? That's my father.

g) ______________________? Sam Smith.

3 Write

I am from Yemen. **My** name's Abed.
You are from Kuwait. **Your** name's Jaber.
He is from Egypt. **His** name's Gamal.
She is from Lebanon. **Her** name's Sabiha.

Write **my**, **your**, **his** or **her** in the spaces.

a) This is my aunt. _____ name's Fatima.

b) "Who's that?"
"That's my cousin. _____ name's Bashir."

c) "Are you Selwa?"
"No. _____ name's Nada."

d) "Is that _____ brother?"
"No. That's my cousin."

4 Write

Who's this?	This is …
Who's that?	That's …
	It's …

Write **this** or **that** in the spaces.

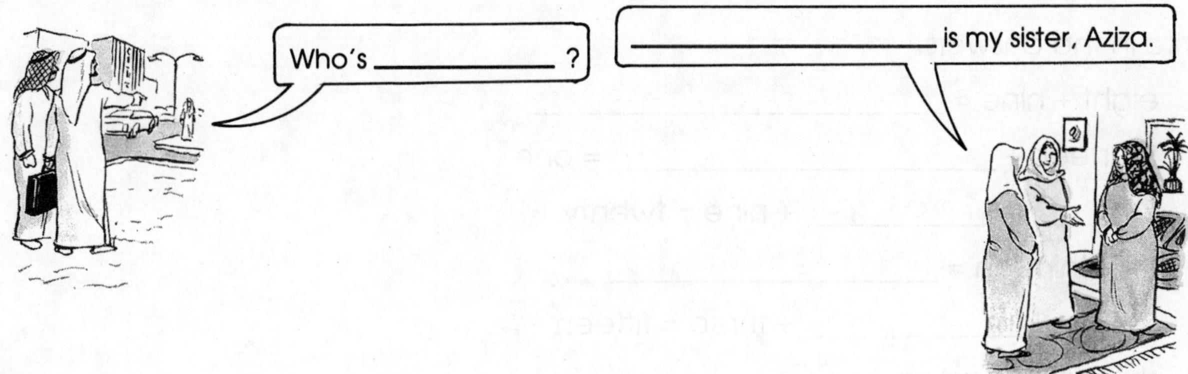

Who's _____________ ?
_____________________ is my sister, Aziza.

5 Match

Match the questions and answers.

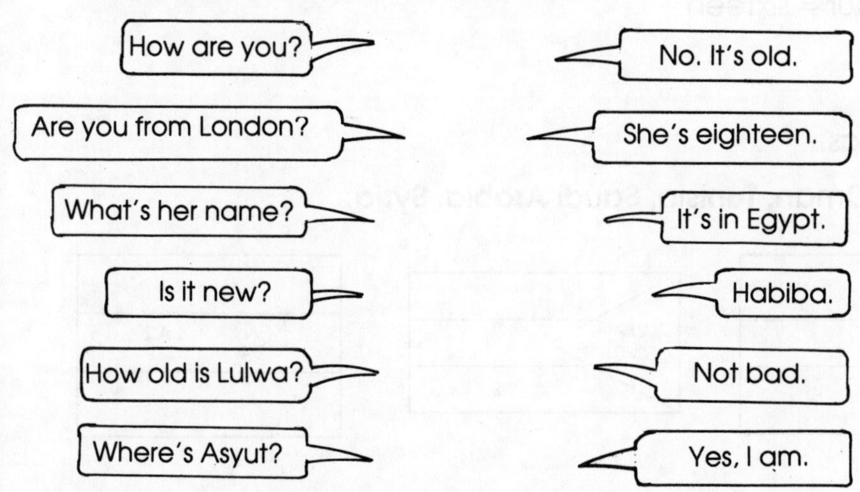

How are you?
Are you from London?
What's her name?
Is it new?
How old is Lulwa?
Where's Asyut?
No. It's old.
She's eighteen.
It's in Egypt.
Habiba.
Not bad.
Yes, I am.

NEW WORDS

6 The family

Write these words in the lists:

aunt, mother, uncle, wife, father, brother, daughter, grandfather, sister, husband.

son	______________
______________	______________
______________	______________
______________	grandmother
______________	______________
______________	______________
cousin	cousin

7 **Numbers** 0–20

Write in the answers.

a) eight + nine = ______________

b) fourteen – ______________ = one

c) ______________ + nine = twenty

d) six + thirteen = ______________

e) ______________ + three = fifteen

f) sixteen – fourteen = ______________

g) ______________ – eleven = seven

h) ______________ – four = sixteen

8 Countries

Match the countries with the flags.

Algeria, Egypt, Jordan, Kuwait, Oman, Tunisia, Saudi Arabia, Syria.

____

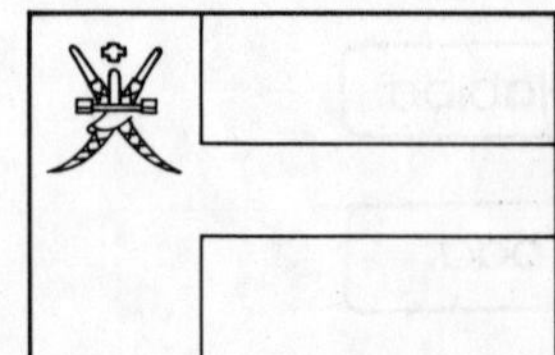
____

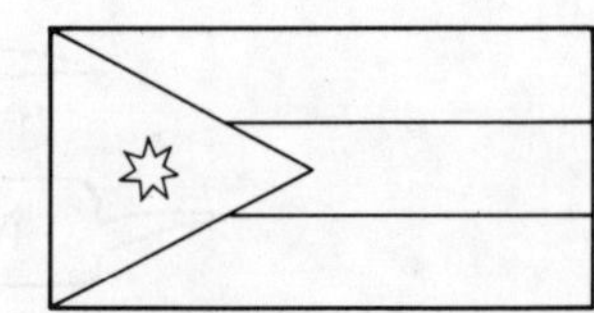
____

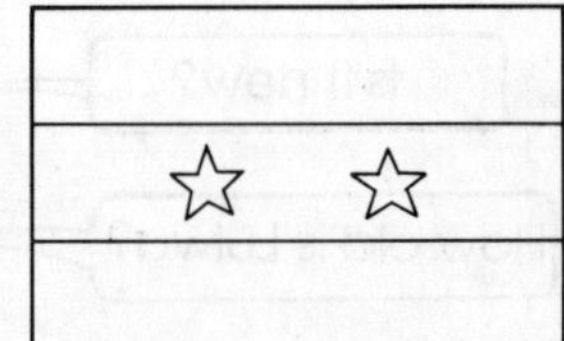
____

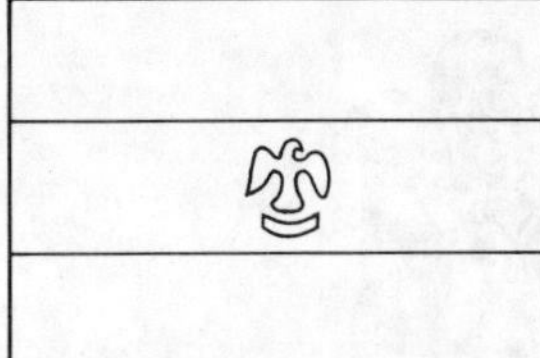
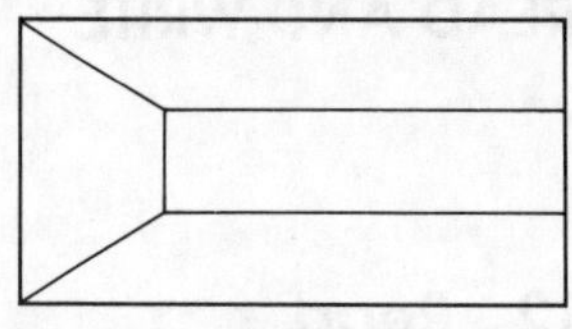

9 Write

Write in the missing words.

Is it good? No. It's bad.

Is it cheap? No. ______.

Is Gary old? No. ______.

Is your car old? No. ______.

Is her house big? No. ______.

Is Mona tall? No. ______.

PUNCTUATION

10 Write

Write the sentences with punctuation (' , . ?) and capital letters.

a) how are you ______

b) my names saleem saeedi ______

c) im from damascus in syria ______

d) its expensive ______

e) wheres mr brown from ______

f) are you from riyadh ______

g) how old is jamila ______

SPELLING

11 Look

Find eight mistakes in these sentences.

a) My naime's Abdullah Mohammad. I'm fram Hofuf in Saudi Arabia.

b) This is my daghter, Samira. She's twalve years old.

c) My frend is from Kerak. That's in Jerdan.

d) This is my hotel. It's viry good and cheep.

READ AND WRITE

12 Read

This is Simon Star. He's twenty-six years old and he's a famous basketball player. He's very rich too! Simon is from Los Angeles in the United States. His wife is also from the United States, but she isn't from Los Angeles. She's from Miami. Her name's Susy. They are in Cairo for a basketball game.

NAME: ______________________	NAME: ______________________
CITY: ______________________	CITY: ______________________
COUNTRY: ______________________	COUNTRY: ______________________

13 Read

Read these sentences:

This is my friend, Warqa. She's from Asyut in Egypt.
This is my uncle, Waleed. He's from Zarqa in Jordan.

Now write sentences with these words:

a) cousin - Nazir - Muscat - Oman

____

b) teacher - Mr Walker - Manchester - England

____

c) aunt - Sabiha - Aleppo - Syria

____

d) friend - Saleem Hashemi - Dammam - Saudi Arabia.

____

____

STORY: HELLO LONDON (1)

Khalid and his grandfather are in Dubai airport.

I'm David Jones.
I'm Khalid and this is my grandfather.

Tea or coffee?
Tea, please.

Oh. I'm sorry!
That's all right.

Here.
Thank you.

Welcome to London!
BRITISH AIRWAYS
HEATHROW

UNIT 3 Jobs and Nationalities

Lesson 1 He's a mechanic

1 Match

a teacher a doctor a student a nurse a mechanic

2 Listen

Write A, B, C or D.

A Hello. How are you?
Not bad, thanks. Are you a nurse?
No, I'm not. I'm a doctor. My name's Salwa.

B That's my cousin.
What's his name?
Salem.
Is he a teacher?
No, he isn't. He's a student.

C This is my friend, Hamid.
Hello, Hamid.
Hello.
He's a mechanic.
Oh! I'm very pleased to meet you!

D Jamila! Look! I'm a spaceman!
No, you're not, Mohsin. You're just a boy.

Write in the jobs.

a) Salwa is ____ __________.

b) Salem is ____ __________.

c) Hamid is ____ __________.

Look!

I'm **a** spaceman
She's **a** doctor.
He's **a** mechanic.
He's **a** student.

3 Listen and say

a teacher a student a doctor a driver

a mechanic a policeman a nurse

Listen again. a tea**ch**er a me**ch**anic

4 What's your job?

I'm … a teacher
a nurse
a student
a mechanic
a driver
a policeman
a doctor
a secretary

I'm __________

I'm __________

I'm __________

I'm __________

I'm __________

I'm __________

I'm __________

I'm __________

5 Ask and answer

Ask five students.

What's your job?

I'm a …
I don't have a job.

Look!

not (n't)

I'm a mechanic. I'm not a mechanic.

I'm a doctor.	I'm **not** a nurse.	I'm not	=	I am not
You're my brother.	You're **not** a spaceman. (You are**n't** a spaceman.)	You're not (You aren't)	=	You are not
He's a student.	He is**n't** a teacher.	He isn't	=	He is not
She's a doctor.	She is**n't** a nurse.	She isn't	=	She is not

6 Match

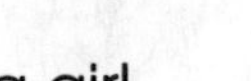

a girl, a woman, a man, a boy,

Now write the words in the spaces.

a) Mohsin is ____ ________________.
b) Jamila is ____ ________________.
c) Salwa is ____ ________________.
d) Hamid is ____ ________________.

Language

a

a student,
a teacher,
a mechanic,
a doctor

I'm a student.
You're a teacher.
He's a mechanic.
She's a doctor.

not

I'm **not** a nurse.
You're **not** a spaceman. You are**n't** a spaceman.
He's **not** a mechanic. He is**n't** a mechanic.

What's your job?
I'm a …
I don't have a job.

Lesson 2 These are my brothers

 **1 Listen**

This is my uncle, Nasser. He's a pilot.
Hello.
Hi.

And these are my brothers, Waleed and Bashir.
How do you do?
Pleased to meet you.

They're students at the Capital English School.

Are you learning English?
I'm sorry. I don't understand.

Write.

a) Nasser is ____ ____________________.

b) Waleed and Bashir are ____________________.

Look!

a student	student**s**
a pilot	pilot**s**
a friend	friend**s**

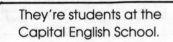

2 Write

Complete the lists.

a doctor	______
______	mechanics
a driver	______
______	teachers
He's a pilot.	They're pilots.
She's a nurse.	They're nurses.

3 Listen and say

sssss student**s**, pilot**s**, mechanic**s**, mosques

zzzzz teacher**s**, girl**s**, boy**s**, drivers

iz nurse**s**, boxe**s**, pages

4 Ask and answer

Introduce two other students like this.

A: **These are my friends, … and …**

B: **Hello. How do you do?**

C and D: **Pleased to meet you.**

Look!

This is my friend.
These are my friends.

5 Listen and say

Say these words:

these, please, meet, evening, three, zero, me, cheap, police, nineteen, he, she.

Say these words:

this, six, in, is, big, it, sister, his, beginner, city.

Look!

they

He's a student.	**They're** students.
She's a student.	(**They are** students.)

6 Write

Write **these, they, a, is, this, my, she** in the spaces.

Latifa: Hello, Sarah.
Sarah: Hello.

Latifa: _______ my sister, Suad.
Sarah: How do you do.
Saud: How do you do.

Latifa: ______'s ______ teacher.

And ______ are ______ friends, Nora and Fawzia.
Sarah: Hello.
Nora and Fawzia: Hello.
Latifa: ______'re students.

Look!

and

These are my brothers Waleed and Bashir.

Language

This is my brother. **These are** my brother**s.**
This is my sister. **These are** my sister**s**.

He's a student. **They're** student**s**.
She's a nurse. **They're** nurse**s**.

I don't understand.

and – Waleed **and** Bashir

Lesson 3 Are you English?

1 Listen

Listen to the receptionist and Bob and Ann.
They are in a hotel.

R: Where are you from, please?
Bob: We're from England.
R: And your nationality? Are you English?
Ann: That's right. English or British.
R: Are you from London?
Ann: No, we're not.
Bob: I'm from Oxford.
R: Where's that?
Bob: It's near London. And my wife's from Leeds.
R: Leeds. How do you spell that?
Ann: L–E–E–D–S

Put a tick (√) or a cross (x).

a) Mr and Mrs Barry are English. ☐

b) They are from London. ☐

c) Ann is from Oxford. ☐

d) Oxford is near London. ☐

e) Bob is from Oxford. ☐

2 Write

Write **where, near, right, Egyptian, from, are** in the spaces.

Where ____ you from?
We're ____ Tanta.
Tanta? ______'s that?
It's _______ Cairo.
Are you ________?
Yes, that's ______.

3 Listen and say

Jordanian Lebanese Kuwaiti

-an	-ese	-i
Jordanian	Lebanese	Kuwaiti
Tunisian	Sudanese	Bahraini
Moroccan		Saudi
Algerian		Emirati
Palestinian		Qatari
Syrian		Yemeni
Egyptian		Omani
Libyan		Iraqi

Look!

I'm from Amman in Jordan. I'm Jordanian.
We're from Beirut in Lebanon. We're Lebanese.
She's from Fehahil in Kuwait. She's Kuwaiti.

4 Match

Match the country and the nationality.

Country	*Nationality*
The United Kingdom	French
Japan	German
France	Dutch
Holland	American
Germany	British
The United States	Japanese

Look!

You

Are you Egyptian?
Yes, I am.

Are you Egyptian?
Yes, we are.

5 Ask and answer

Who am I?

Ask and answer with a friend.

Choose:

a singer, a politician, an actor

Are you ...? — No I'm not. / Yes, I am.

Are you a man? Yes, I am.
Are you Egyptian? No, I'm not.
Are you American? Yes, I am.
Are you a singer? No, I'm not.
Are you a politician? Yes, I am.
Are you Bill Clinton? Yes, I am.

6 Listen and say

Numbers 20–30:

20 – **twenty** 21 – **twenty-one** 22 – **twenty-two**
23 – **twenty-three** 24 – **twenty-four** 25 – **twenty-five**
26 – **twenty-six** 27 – **twenty-seven** 28 – **twenty-eight**
29 – **twenty-nine** 30 – **thirty**

How old are you? I'm twenty-two.
I'm twenty-two years old.

Language

We are English. nationality
We are from England. country

Are **you** English? Yes, **I am**. numbers 21–30
Are **you** English? Yes, **we are**.

near

How old are you? I'm twenty-two **years old**.

Lesson 4 Where are we?

1 Match

hungry, hot, tired, cold, thirsty.

2 Listen

Where are we?
I don't know.
Are we near Amman?
Yes, I think we are.
I'm tired.
So am I... and I'm hungry, too.
Have an orange.
Thanks.

3 Match

Match the questions and the answers.

a)	Where are Sarah and Latifa?	Yes, she is.
b)	Are they tired?	They're on a bus.
c)	Is Latifa hungry?	It's near Amman.
d)	Where is the bus?	Yes, they are.

Look!

Questions.

We are near Amman.	Are we near Amman? Where are we?
They are tired.	Are they tired?

Look!

not (n't)

We're hungry.	We're not hungry. We aren't hungry.
They're tired.	They're not tired. They aren't tired.

4 Write

Write about these people.

a) 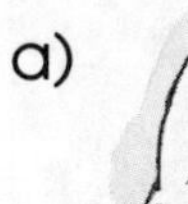 He's happy.

b)  ______________________

c)  ______________________

d)  ______________________

e)  ______________________

f)  ______________________

5 Listen and say

we're, near

they're, where

> **Look!**
>
> Have **an** o̲range.
>
> Have **a** sandwich.

6 Ask and answer

Are you thirsty?
tired?
cold?
hungry?
Have a ...
jacket

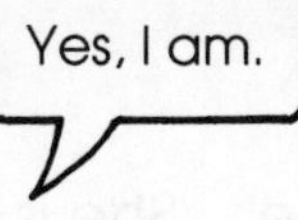

7 Listen

Write A, B, C or D.

_______ _______ _______ _______

Really? Really! Really! Really.

Language

an - **an** orange

Are we …?
We're not …
We aren't …

Are they …?
They're not …
They aren't …

I think …

So am I.

Really?

STUDY

The verb: **to be**

I	I am I'm	I'm from Lebanon. I'm Lebanese. I'm not Jordanian.
		Are you Lebanese? Yes, I am. Are you Jordanian? No, I'm not.
You	You are You're	You're from England. You're English. You're not French. You aren't French.
		Am I late? Yes, you are. No, you aren't. (No, you're not.)
He	He is He's	He's from Saudi Arabia. He's Saudi. He's not Kuwaiti. He isn't Kuwaiti.
		Is he Saudi? Yes, he is. Is he Kuwaiti? No, he isn't.
She	She is She's	She's from Oman. She's Omani. She's not Bahraini. She isn't Bahraini.
		Is she Omani? Yes, she is. Is she Bahraini. No, she isn't.

It	It is It's	It's near London.
We	We are We're	We're from Egypt. We're Egyptian. We're not Tunisian. We aren't Tunisian. Are we late? Yes, we are. No, we aren't.

They	They are They're	They're from Morocco. They're Moroccan. They're not Algerian. They aren't Algerian. Are they Moroccan? Yes, they are. Are they Algerian? No, they aren't.

---

a I'm a doctor.
He's a student.

They're nurses.

Have a sandwich. Thanks.
an orange.

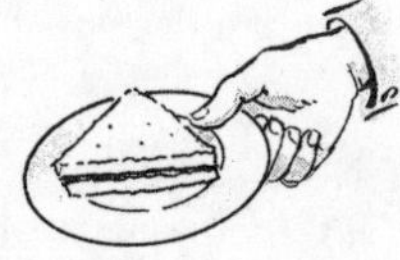

What's your job?	I'm a clerk.
What's your nationality?	I'm Lebanese.

---

don't I don't have a job.
I don't know.
I don't understand.
I don't speak English.

I think …
I know.
Really?

I'm hungry. **So am I.**

This is my brother.	He's **a** student.
These are my brothers.	They're student**s**.

How old are you? I'm twenty-three **years old**.

NEW WORDS

Learn these words.

jobs

a mechanic
a nurse
a doctor
a student
a teacher
a spaceman
a driver
a policeman
a secretary
a basketball player
a politician
an actor

nationalities

Algerian
American
Bahraini
British
Dutch
Egyptian
English
Emirati
French
German
Iraqi
Japanese
Jordanian
Kuwaiti
Libyan
Moroccan
Omani
Palestinian
Qatari
Saudi
Sudanese
Syrian
Tunisian
Yemeni

people

a man
a woman
a boy
a girl

things

a sandwich
a seat
an orange

adjectives

hot
cold
hungry
thirsty
tired

countries

Bahrain
France
Germany
Holland
Iraq
Japan
Lebanon
Morocco
Qatar
Sudan

The United Arab Emirates
The United Kingdom
Yemen

numbers 21–30

twenty-one
twenty-two
twenty-three
twenty-four
twenty-five
twenty-six
twenty-seven
twenty-eight
twenty-nine
thirty

UNIT 4 In the City

Lesson 1 What's that?

1 Read

Gary and Mohammad are in a taxi.

What's that, Mohammad?
It's the royal palace.
Oh. It's beautiful.
Yes it is. It's very old.

And what's that?
What?

That new building, there.
What is it?
Sorry. I don't know.

It's a bank. The Gulf Bank.
Really? It's very big.

Write the words: **new, big, old**.

a) The royal palace is very __________.

b) The bank is __________.

c) The bank is very __________.

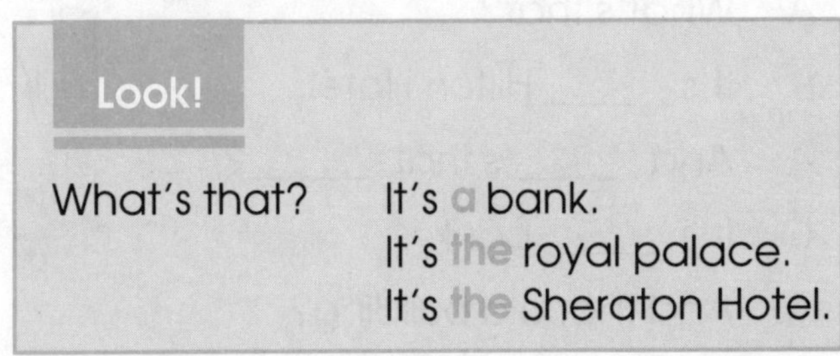

Look!

What's that? It's a bank.
It's the royal palace.
It's the Sheraton Hotel.

2 Ask and answer

A

B

What's that? It's a …
I don't know.

3 Ask and answer

What's that? **It's the …**
(I don't know.)

Where is it? **It's in …**

4 Write

Write **that, don't, a, what, there, the** in the spaces.

A: What's that?

B: It's ______ Hilton Hotel.

A: And ______'s that, ______?

C: It's ______ bank.

A: And that old building?

B: Sorry. I _______ know.

C: _______'s a hospital.

5 Write

Write **a**, or **an** in the spaces.

_____ building, _____ ice-cream,
_____ new school, _____ jacket,
_____ car, _____ expensive watch,
_____ house, _____ key,
_____ umbrella, _____ orange.

> **Look!**
>
> It's a watch. It's **an** orange.
>
> It's a car.
> It's a new car.
> It's **an** expensive car.
>
> We write **an** before **a, e, i, o, u.**

Match the pictures with the words above.

a)

b)

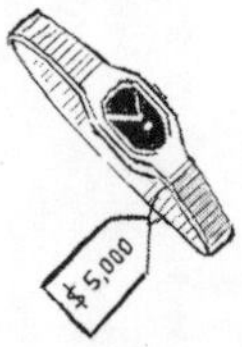

c)

d)

e)

f)

i)

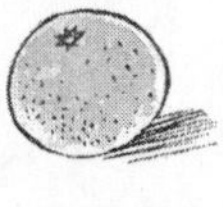
j)

k)

l)

6 Listen and say

where, they're, there
we're, near, here

Listen

A: Look!
B: Where?
A: There.
B: Oh, yes. They're beautiful.

Listen

A: We're here.
B: Near the school?
A: No. Near the hotel.
B: That's good. We're tired.

> **Language**
>
> It's a bank.
> It's **the** Bank of Bahrain.
>
> It's a hotel.
> It's **the** Sheraton Hotel.
>
> It's a house. It's **the** royal palace.
>
> **an** expensive car
>
> It's a bank. It's beautiful.
>
> It's **a beautiful bank**.
>
> there, here

Lesson 2 Is it far?

1 Listen and write

Write A, B or C in the boxes.

Excuse me, where's the Capital English School?

It's near the mosque.

Is it far?

No, not far. It's about half a kilometre.

Selwa, where's the Bank of Bahrain?

It's next to the Meridian Hotel.

Where's that?

It's not far from the market.

Excuse me, where's the KOC building?

Pardon?

The KOC building?

It's there, look.

Oh yes. Thanks.

Look!

next to

near
not far from

2 Ask and answer

A	B
Where's the market?	It's near the airport.
the Habib Bank?	the school.
the hospital?	the mosque.
the police station?	the royal palace.
the Good Luck Hotel?	the Kuwaiti Building.

mosque
airport
market
police station
Kuwaiti Building
hospital
Habib Bank
royal palace
Good Luck Hotel
school

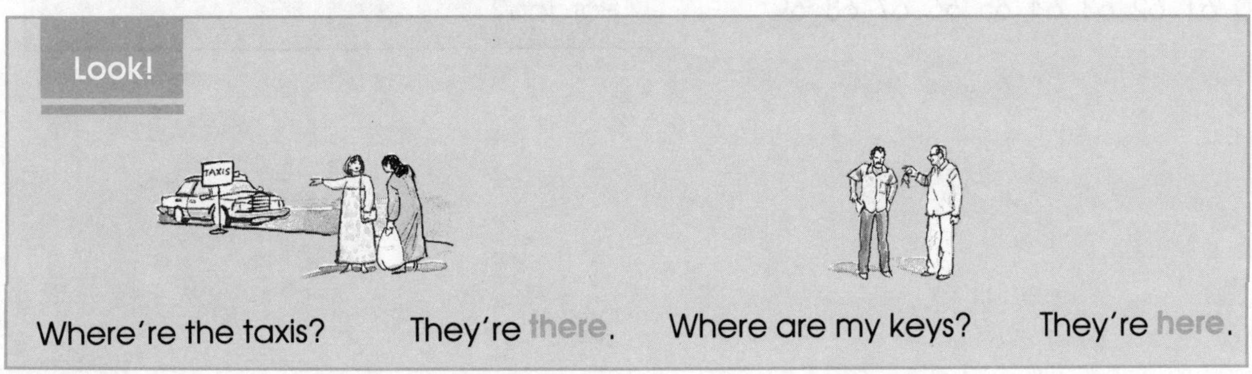

Look!

Where're the taxis? They're **there**. Where are my keys? They're **here**.

3 Write

Write **airport**, **the**, **pardon**, **about**, **next**, **far**, **excuse**, **where**, **not** in the spaces.

A: ____________ me, ____________'s the airport?

B: ____________ ?

A: Where's the ______________ ?

B: It's ____________ to ____________ hospital.

A: Is it ____________ ?

B: ____________ far. It's ____________ one kilometre.

4 Listen and say

Where's the bus station?
What's your name?
How old are you?

Is it far?
Are you from London?
Are they American?

5 Listen and say

Numbers 30–69:

30 – **thirty** 31 – **thirty-one** 32 – **thirty-two** …
40 – **forty** 41 – **forty-one** 42 – **forty-two** …
50 – **fifty** 51 – **fifty-one** 52 – **fifty-two** …
60 – **sixty** 61 – **sixty-one** 62 – **sixty-two** …

6 Listen

Circle the number you hear.

30 31 (32) 33 34 35 36 37 38 39

40 41 42 43 44 45 46 47 48 49

50 51 52 53 54 55 56 57 58 59

60 61 62 63 64 65 66 67 68 69

Language

next to
not far from

Is it far?
Where's the …?

Excuse me.
Pardon?

Lesson 3 The market

1 Listen

Sarah: What are those, please?
Khalifa: They're dates. Have one.
Sarah: Thanks. They're sweet.
Latifa: How much are they?
Khalifa: Two rials for a kilo.
Sarah: Er . . . Half a kilo, please.
Latifa: And are these lemons?
Khalifa: Yes, that's right. There're one rial for one kilo.
Sarah: OK. One kilo, please.

Find the answer.

Sarah pays
a) one rial
b) two rials
c) three rials
d) one and a half rials

for the dates and lemons.

2 Match

a) 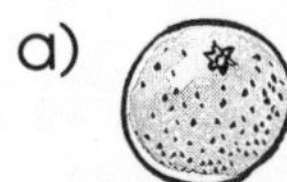 b) 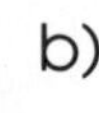  c)   d)  e) 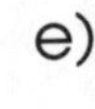  f) 

a banana, a watermelon, an apple, an orange, a lemon, a date.

Look!

What's this?	It's a lemon.
What're these?	They're lemons.
What's that?	It's a date.
What're those?	They're dates.

3 Ask and answer

A	B
What's this?	It's a lemon.
What are these?	They're dates

    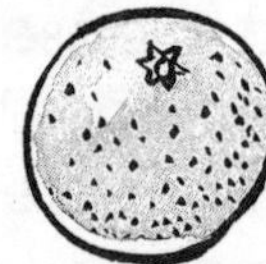 

Look!

dirham, dollar, pound, rial, dinar.

a kilo

They're five rials a kilo.
(They're five rials for one kilo.)

4 Ask and answer

How much is this radio?	**It's 50 dinars.**
How much are these dates?	**They're one rial a kilo.**

A

B

5 Write

Write **much**, **sweet**, **these**, **they**, **expensive**, **are ('re)**, **very**, **dirhams** in the spaces.

A: What are ______________?

B: They ______________ apricots.

A: Are ______________ nice?

B: Yes, they're ______________ nice and ______________.

A: How ______________ are they?

B: 20 ______________ a kilo.

A: They're ______________!

6 Listen and say

those, know, no, old, cold, don't

A: What are those?
B: Those?
A: No. Not those. Those!
B: Ah. Those. I don't know.

> **Language**
>
> What are these? / What are those?
>
> These apples are … / Those dates are …
>
> How much is …? / How much are …?

Lesson 4 Streets and roads

AL-ISTIQLAL STREET

1 Read and match

a) Excuse me. Is this the road to the airport? — Yes, it is.

b) What's the problem? — It's the clutch.

c) Super or normal? — Super, please. Full.

d) Is this King Faisal Street? — No, it's Al Istiqlal Street.

Look!

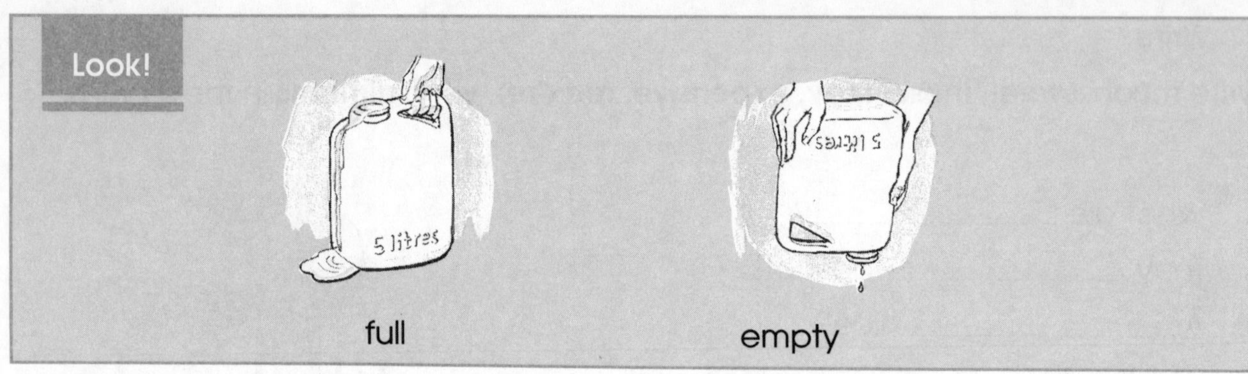

full empty

2 Match

Write the words under the pictures.

a garage, a lorry, a bicycle, a street, a bus station, a car, a road, a bus, a taxi, a petrol station.

a)  ____________

b)  ____________

c)  ____________

d) 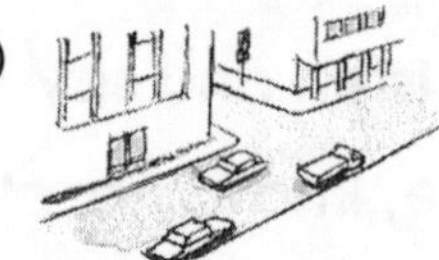 ____________

e)  ____________

f)  ____________

g)  ____________

h) 

____

i)  ____________

j)  ____________

3 Write

Write the words in the dialogue:

much, next, mosque, where, dinars, please, it.

A: Taxi!

B: Yes?

A: Momtaz Hotel, __________ .

Look!

American English	*British English*
gas	petrol
truck	lorry
cab	taxi

B: ____________'s that?

A: _____'s in King Faisal Street. __________ to the ___________ .

B: Yes, I know.

A: How ____________ is it?

B: Two _______________ .

A: All right.

4 Ask and answer

A	B
Taxi!	**Yes.**
Cairo Street, please.	**Where's that?**
Near the park.	**I know.**
How much is it?	**… dinars.**
All right.	

Ask for:		
	Beirut Street	– near the bus station.
	The Palace Hotel	– near the airport
	The Habib Bank	– near the hospital
	Tunis Street	– near the royal palace

5 Listen and say

Numbers 70–100:

70 – **seventy** 71 – **seventy-one** 72 – **seventy-two** …
80 – **eighty** 81 – **eighty-one** 82 – **eighty-two** …
90 – **ninety** 91 – **ninety-one** 92 – **ninety-two** …
100 – **a hundred**

6 Listen and say

sh sta**ti**on, na**ti**onality, Engli**sh**, **Sh**eraton.
tsh mu**ch**, wa**tch**, **ch**eap, clu**tch**, sandwi**ch**.

What's the problem?
I think it's the brakes.

Language

What's the problem? It's …

Is this … ? Yes, it is.
No, it isn't.

Is this the road to …?

I know.

STUDY

It's **a** bank.  It's **the** Bank of Bahrain.

It's **a** house.  It's **the** airport.

an – before **a, e, i, o, u.**

an **a**pple, an **e**xpensive car, an **i**ce-cream, an **o**range, an **u**mbrella.

It's a beautiful building. They're beautiful buildings.
It's a sweet orange. They're sweet oranges.

there 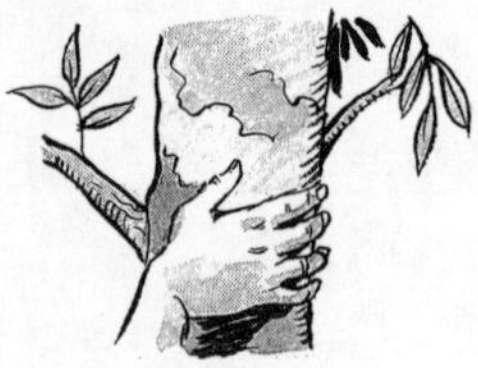 here 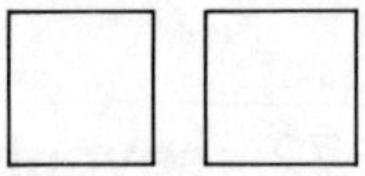 next to not far from

this, that, these, those

What'**s this**? It's a lemon.
What'**re these**? They're lemons.

What'**s that**? It's a date.
What'**re those**? They're dates.

How much How much is it? How much are they?

What's the problem?

Is this the road to …? Yes, it is. No, it isn't.

NEW WORDS

Learn these words.

places	*in the city*	*shopping*	*adjectives*
a building	a road	a watermelon	sweet
a royal palace	a street	an apricot	fresh
a school	a lorry (truck)	dates	full
a hospital	a taxi (cab)	a banana	empty
a hotel	a bicycle	a lemon	
a bank	brakes	a kilo	
a house	clutch		
a market	a kilometre		
an airport			
a park			
a bus station			
a petrol (gas) station			

numbers

thirty, forty, fifty, sixty, seventy, eighty, ninety, a hundred.

Review Unit B

GRAMMAR

1 Write

I am …
You are …
He is …
She is …
It is …
We are …
They are …

Write **am, are** or **is** in the spaces.

Waleed and Bashir ________ students at the Capital English School. They __________ Bahraini. Waleed ________ from Jidhafs, a small town near Manama, and Bashir ___________ from Muharraq. The school ________in Manama.

My name ___________ Khalifa Ben Yahya. I __________ from Sfax in Tunisia.My wife's name ____________ Afifa. She ___________ also from Sfax. We _________ Tunisian. I ________________ an officer in the army and my wife ____________ a teacher.

2 Answer

Am I …?	Yes, you are.	No, you aren't.
Are you …?	Yes, I am.	No, I'm not.
Is he …?	Yes, he is.	No, he isn't.
Is she …?	Yes, she is.	No, she isn't.
Is it …?	Yes, it is.	No, it isn't.
Are we …?	Yes, we are.	No, we aren't.
Are they …?	Yes, they are.	No, they aren't.

Answer these questions:

a) Are your friends from Sudan?

No, ______________ . They're Egyptian.

b) Is Omar Kuwaiti? No, ________________ . He's Bahraini.

c) Are Samia and Fawzia from Tunisia? Yes, ________________ .

d) Is Selwa Egyptian?

No, ________________ . ________________ Palestinian.

e) Are you Moroccan? No, ________________ . ____________ Algerian.

f) Is Latifa Omani? Yes, ________________ .

g) Are Waleed and Bashir from Syria?

No, ______________ . ______________ from Bahrain.

h) Is Salah Lebanese? Yes, ________________ .

i) Is Zainah Yemeni?

No, ______________ . ______________ from Saudi Arabia.

Now answer this question.

j) Are you English?

No, ______________ . ____________________________ .

3 Write

It's a bank. It's the Bank of Bahrain.
It's a hotel. It's the Good Luck Hotel.

Where's the market? Where's the airport?

She's a teacher. He's a teacher. They're teachers.

an apple, an English book, an ice-cream, an orange, an umbrella.

Write **a**, **an**, **the** or **(-)**.

a) "Where's ______ Capital English School, please?"

"It's near ______ airport."

b) "Is he _______ singer?" "No, he's ________ actor."

c) "It's ___________ beautiful car."

"Yes, but it's ____________ expensive car too!"

d) "What's that?"

"It's ________ watermelon. It's very sweet."

"And what are those?"

"They're ______ apricots."

e) "What's that building, there? Is it __________ bank?"

"No. It's _______ hotel. It's __________ Palace Hotel. It's _________ new."

4 Write

It's a building. It's tall.	They're dates. They're sweet.
It's a tall building.	**They're sweet dates.**
The building is tall.	**The dates are sweet.**

Change the sentences.

a) It's a big watermelon.

The watermelon _____ big.

b) They're expensive cameras.

The ________________________.

c) They're old men.

The ________________________.

d) It's a beautiful park.

The ________________________.

e) It's a new house.

The ________________________.

f) They're nice sandwiches.

The ________________________.

5 Write

Write **this**, **that**, **these**, or **those** in the spaces.

How much are ____________________?

How much is ____________________?

How much are ____________________?

How much is ____________________?

NEW WORDS

6 Nationalities

Write in the nationalities.

Country	Nationality	Country	Nationality
Algeria	______________ .	Saudi Arabia	______________ .
Bahrain	______________ .	Sudan	______________ .
Egypt	______________ .	Syria	______________ .
Iraq	______________ .	Tunisia	______________ .
Jordan	______________ .	The United Arab Emirates	______________ .
Kuwait	______________ .	Yemen	______________ .
Lebanon	______________ .	France	______________ .
Libya	______________ .	Germany	______________ .
Morocco	______________ .	Holland	______________ .
Oman	______________ .	Japan	______________ .
Palestine	______________ .	The United Kingdom	______________ .
Qatar	______________ .	The United States	______________ .

7 Places

What are these places in the city? Write: **airport**, **royal palace**, **hotel**, **park**, **street**, **road**, **bank**, **house**, **market**, **bus station**, **school**, **mosque**, **petrol station**.

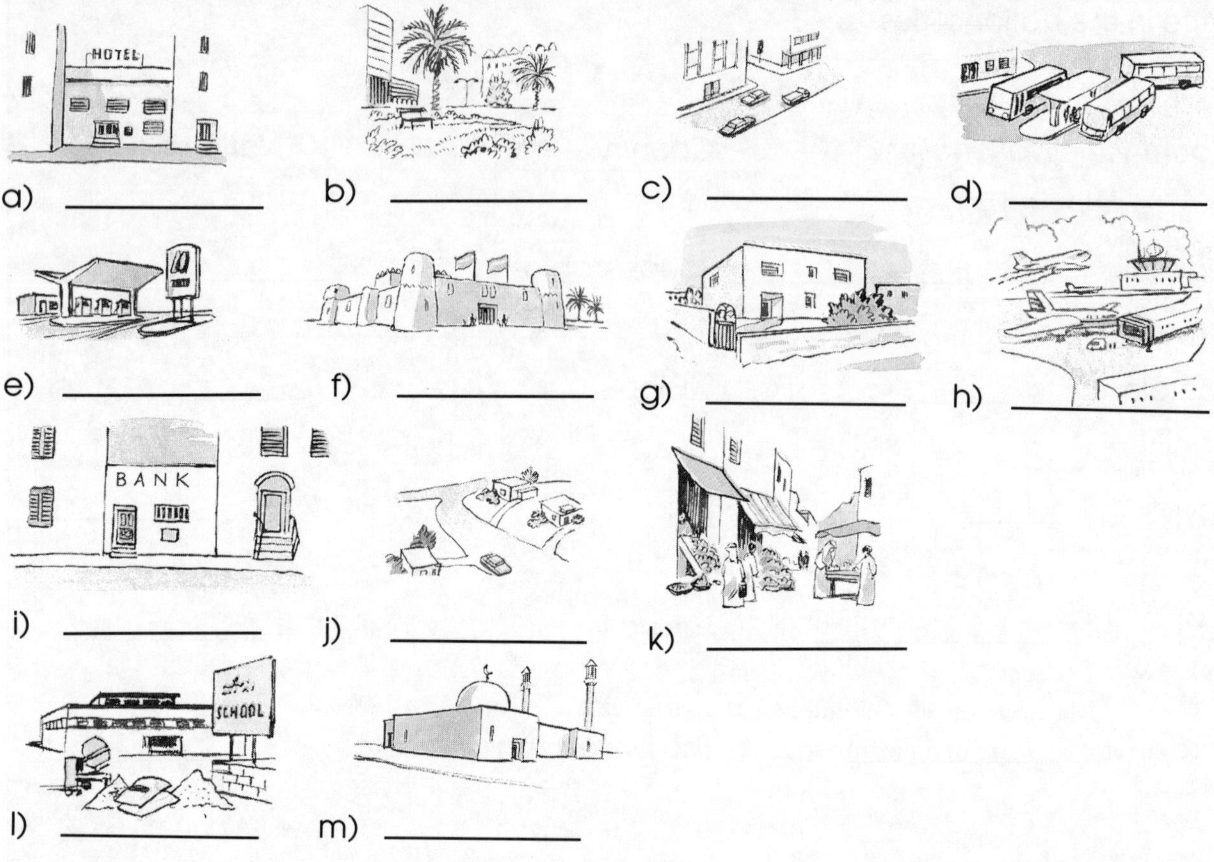

a) ________ b) ________ c) ________ d) ________

e) ________ f) ________ g) ________ h) ________

i) ________ j) ________ k) ________

l) ________ m) ________

8 Jobs

What are these jobs? Write: **teacher**, **driver**, **student**, **mechanic**, **policeman**, **secretary**, **doctor**, **nurse**, **pilot**, **singer**, **actor**, **politician**, **spaceman**.

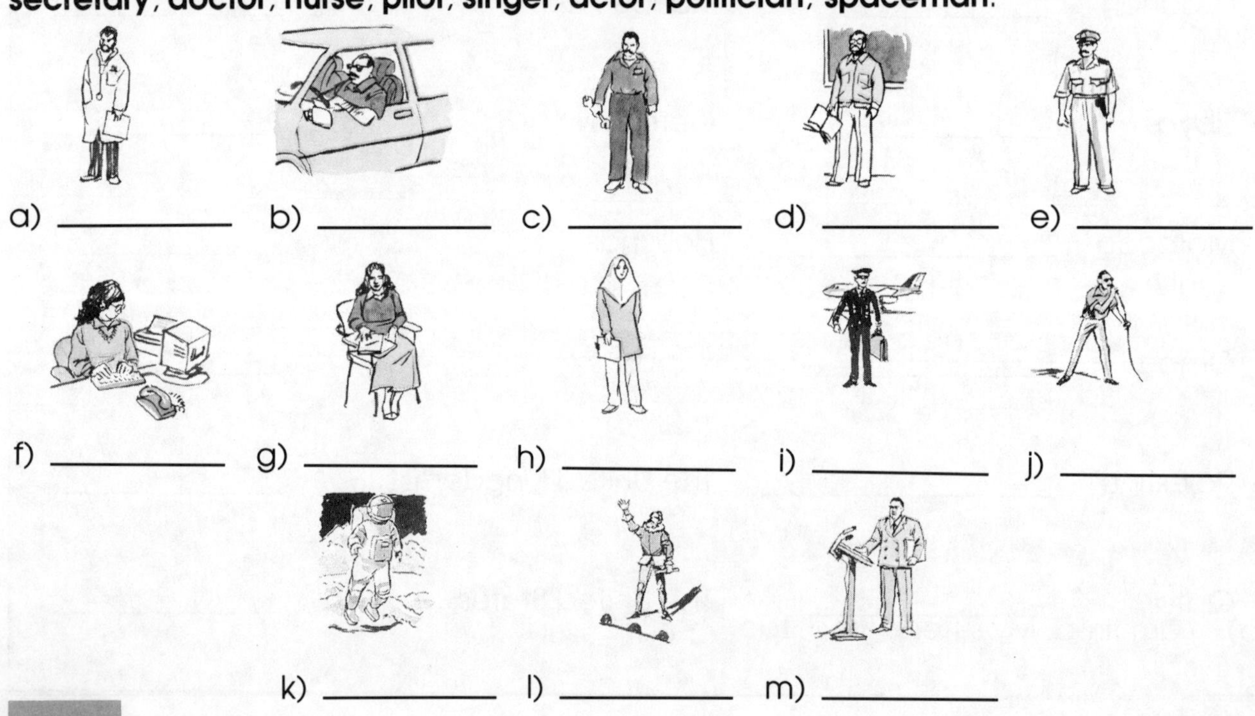

a) ________ b) ________ c) ________ d) ________ e) ________

f) ________ g) ________ h) ________ i) ________ j) ________

k) ________ l) ________ m) ________

PUNCTUATION

9 Write

Write these sentences with punctuation (' , . ?) and capital letters.

a) theyre lebanese ______________________________

b) wheres the bank of egypt ______________________________

c) its not far from the gulf hotel ______________________________

d) is this al istiqlal street ______________________________

e) whatre those ______________________________

f) im not french im german ______________________________

SPELLING

10 Look

Find 18 spelling mistakes.

My naime's Aziza Jassim and I'm a studant at teh Gulf English Scool.
I'm from Dubai in the Unitd Arab Emirates.
My husbend is a driaver. He issn't from Dubi. He's fram Sharjah.
My hose is very smal, but it's viry nice. It's in Cairo Streat.
It's naxt to a new mosqe. It's not fur from the aireport.

READ AND WRITE

11 Read

Read this paragraph and write **but** and **and** in the sentences.

The Palace Hotel is in Garden City in Cairo. It's very near the River Nile ________ it is next to a small park. The hotel is very beautiful, ________ it is not expensive. A room in the hotel is about $30 a night. The hotel manager is Egyptian. His name is Samir Awad ________ he is from Alexandria.

12 Write

Join these sentences with **and** or **but**.

a) I am tired. My sister is tired, too.

b) I am from Bahrain. My wife is from Saudi Arabia.

c) The jacket is nice. It's very expensive.

d) My name is Selwa Jassim. I am from Fehahil in Kuwait.

e) The new airport is beautiful. It's very far from the city.

f) My cousin is 28 years old. He's a mechanic in a garage.

g) My grandfather is old. He's a good driver.

13 Write

Write about this hotel.

Nasser Hotel – small hotel – centre – Amman / King Faisal Street – near– a mosque / nice – not expensive / manager – Jordanian / Rashid – from Aquaba

STORY: HELLO LONDON

The next day.

Look! That's a nice hotel.
It isn't a hotel. That's Buckingham Palace.

OXFORD STREET
How much are these?
LONDON
LONDON
Five pounds.

What's that?
That's Big Ben.

UNDERGROUND
Ninety pence, please.
London
UNDERGROUND
Pay here

Let's have some tea.
FORUM HOTEL
Yes, I'm thirsty.

UNIT 5 What's it like?

Lesson 1 That's mine!

1 Listen

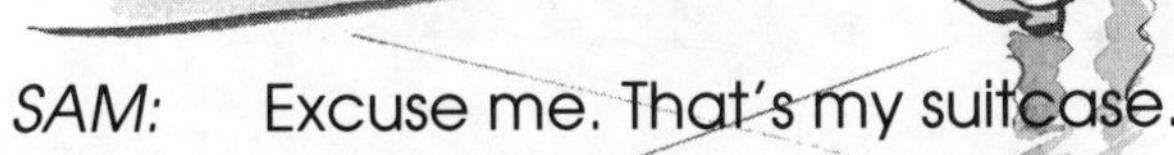

SAM: Excuse me. That's my suitcase.

TOM: No, it isn't. It's our suitcase.

SAM: Well, where's mine?

MARY: What's it like?

SAM: It's black with a red handle.

TOM: I think that's yours – over there.

SAM: Hey. That's my suitcase!

Find Sam's suitcase!

a) b) c) d)

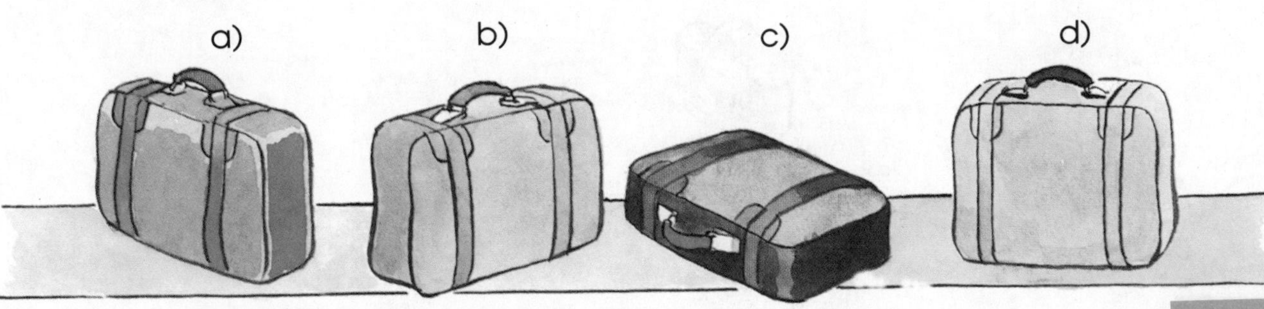

2 Match

What's it like?

a) It's blue and white.
b) It's brown with a black handle.
c) It's green with small wheels.
d) It's small and it's red.
e) It's very big. It's brown and white.
f) It's red with a black handle.

Look!

That's my suitcase.	That's mine.
That's your suitcase.	That's yours.

3 Ask and answer

That's my ... **No, it isn't. It's mine!**

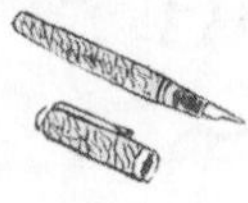

Is this my ...? **Yes, it's yours.**

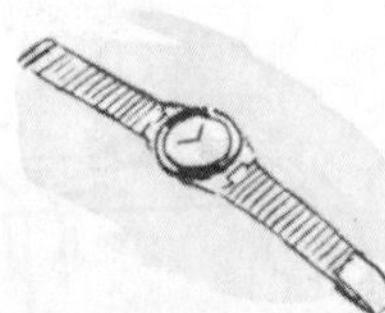

4 Write

Write **like**, **my**, **your**, **yours**, **mine**, **that**, **black** in the spaces.

A: Excuse me. Is this ____________ camera?

B: No, it's not __________ .

A: What's your camera ____________ ?

B: ____________ camera's small and ____________ .

A: Ah. I think this is ______________ .

B: Yes. ________________ 's it. Thank you very much.

5 Write

What colour is it?

It's black.

a)  ________________________________

b) 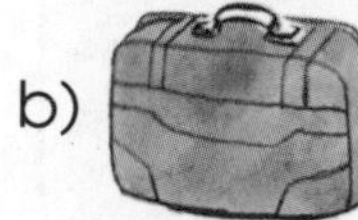 ________________________________

c)  ________________________________

What colour are they?

They're green.

d)  ________________________________

e)  ________________________________

f)  ________________________________

6 Write

What is it?	**It's** a black suitcase.
What are they?	**They're** black suitcase**s**.

a)  It's a black suitcase.

b)  They're red cars.

c) 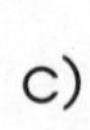  ____________________

d)  ____________________

e)  ____________________

f)  ____________________

g) ____________________

Look!

our, their

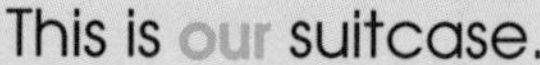

This is **our** suitcase.

That's **their** suitcase.

7 Listen and say

blue, **black**, **brown**, **green**, **small**.

Sounds and spelling

white, **wh**eels, **wh**ere, **wh**en, **wh**y, **wh**at.

Language

It's my suitcase.
It's mine.

It's your suitcase.
It's yours.

It's our suitcase. It's their suitcase.

What's it like?
What colour is it?
What colour are they?

Lesson 2 Whose is this?

1 Read and match

a) Is that his? No, I think it's hers.

b) Whose car is this? It's my brother's.

c) Is this yours? No, it's theirs.

d) Whose is this? It's ours.

Look!

's

Whose car is this?	It's my brother**'s**.
	It's Khalifa**'s**.
	It's Samia**'s**.

2 Ask and answer

Whose ... is this? **It's ... 's.**
Whose ... are these? **They're ... 's.**

Look!

That's	my your his her our their	suitcase.	That's	mine. yours. his. hers. ours. theirs.
That's	Sam's	suitcase.	That's	Sam's.

3 Write

Write **mine**, **yours**, **his**, **hers**, **ours**, **theirs** in the spaces.

a) That's Mr and Mrs Brown's room. It's _________ .

b) This book is Ahmed's. It's ___________ .

c) Look. My name is in the book. It's _________, not yours!

d) This is our house. It's _________ .

e) That's Mariam's handbag. It's __________ .

f) Have this seat. It's not mine, it's __________ .

4 Ask and answer

Is that Latifa's ...? **Yes, it is.**
No. I think it's her ...

5 Match

passport, visa, ticket, money, suitcase, handbag.

a) 

b) 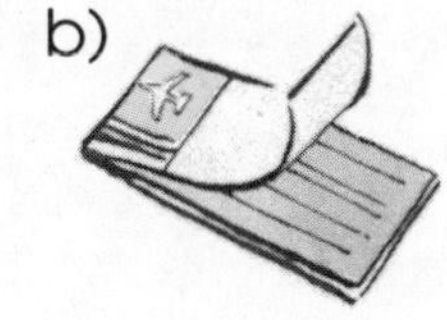

c) 

d) 

e)

f) 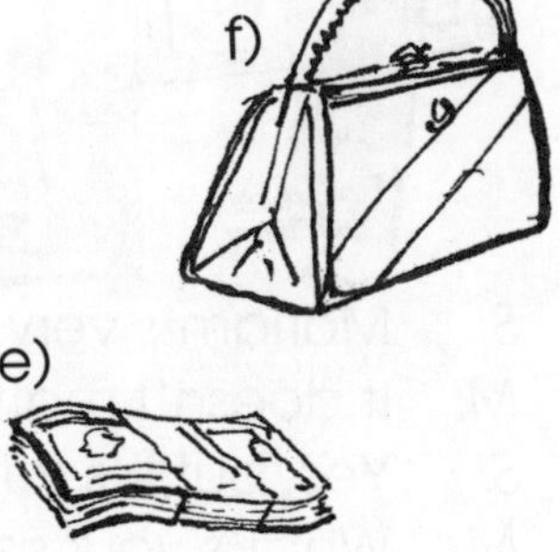

6 Listen and say

who, who's, whose,
blue, two, you, fruit, student, new, suitcase.

Language

Whose is this?	It's mine.
Whose car is this?	yours.
	his.
	hers.
	ours.
	theirs.
	It's Latifa's.

Lesson 3 She's got green eyes

1 Listen

Selwa and Mary are at the airport. They are with Selwa's brother, Awad.

S: Mariam's very late.
M: It doesn't matter.
S: Yes, but it's ten o' clock.
M: What's your sister like?
A: She's quite tall and thin.
M: Like you.
A: Yes. And she's got black hair and green eyes.
M: Green eyes. Really?
S: Yes, beautiful green eyes.
M: How old is she?
S: She's 22.
A: Look. There she is! Mariam ...!

2 Look

Which one is Mariam – a, b, c or d?

a)

b)

c)

d)

Look!

has got

What's she like?
She's got green eyes. She has got green eyes.

What's he like?
He's got black hair. He has got black hair.

3 Match

a) He's tall and thin.
b) She's short and fat.
c) They're short and thin.
d) They're tall and fat.

4 Match

a) He's got short, black hair and brown eyes.
b) He's got brown hair and blue eyes.
c) He's got grey hair and brown eyes. He's got a moustache.
d) He's got fair hair and blue eyes.
e) He's got a beard and a moustache.

f) She's got long blonde hair and green eyes.
g) She's got short, grey hair.
h) She's got black hair and brown eyes.
i) She's got long black hair and blue eyes.

5 Write

Write the words **right**, **brown**, **tall**, **like**, **short**, **got**, **he** in the spaces.

A: What's Simon Star ________ ?
B: He's ____________ big __________ eyes.
A: And his hair?
B: It's __________ and black.
A: Is ____________ tall?
B: Not very ____________ – but he's not short.
A: Medium?
B: That's ___________ .

Look! quite, very

He's very tall.
He's tall.
He's quite tall.
He's not very tall.
He's short.

6 A game

Who is he? Who is she?

Choose someone in the room.

She's …	**He's …**
She's got ….. eyes/hair.	**He's got ….. eyes/hair.**
	a beard.
	a moustache.

Language

What's he like?
What's she like?

She's got … hair.
He's got … eyes.

quite / very / not very

It doesn't matter.

What's the time?
It's … o' clock.

7 Listen and say

Silent letters

The **r** is silent. fai**r**, hai**r** – She's got fai**r** hai**r**.
matte**r**, brothe**r**, siste**r**, sho**r**t.

What's your father like?
He's tall and he's got grey hair.
Eyes?
Yes, he's got two.

Lesson 4 How many?

1 Listen

Mohammad and Gary are having tea in the company canteen.

G: Are you married, Mohammad?
M: Yes, I am.
G: How many children have you got?
M: I've got five. Two boys and three girls.
G: How old are they?
M: The boys are six and two and a half.
G: And your daughters – how old are they?
M: They're seven and four – and Amna – she's just a baby.
G: How old is she?
M: Ten months.

Put a tick (√) or a cross (x)

a) Mohammad has got five children. ☐
b) He has got two sons. ☐
c) He has got two daughters. ☐
d) He has got a baby daughter. ☐
e) Amna is four years old. ☐

Look!

How many children have you got?

I'**ve** got five.
I **have** got five.

child – children

I've got one child.
I've got five children.

2 Ask and answer

How many … have you got?

I've got …
I haven't got any …

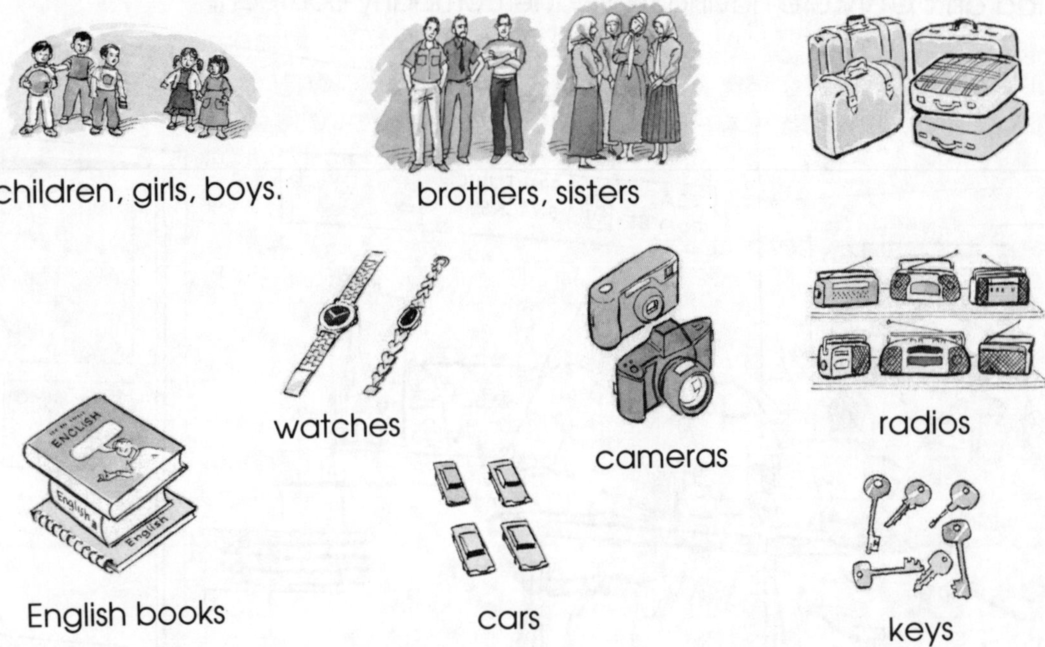

3 Write

Write the words **they**, **got**, **old**, **many**, **eight**, **have**, **girls** in the spaces.

Selwa: How ____________ children ____________ you got?

Mary: I've ____________ three - a boy and two ____________ .

Selwa: How ____________ is the boy?

Mary: He's ____________ .

Selwa: And the girls?

Mary: ____________ 're five and three.

Look!

Are you **married**? Yes, I am.
No, I'm not. I'm **single**

4 Listen

Complete the form.

IMMIGRATION FORM

FIRST NAME: ____________ FAMILY NAME: ____________
CITY: ____________ COUNTRY: ____________
NATIONALITY: ____________
MARRIED/SINGLE: ____________
NO. OF CHILDREN : ____________
ADDRESS IN JORDAN: ____________

5 Listen and say

Numbers 100–200:

100 – **a hundred** 101 – **a hundred and one** 110 – **a hundred and ten**
120 – **a hundred and twenty** 135 – **a hundred and thirty-five**
148 – **a hundred and forty-eight** 153 – **a hundred and fifty-three**
169 – **a hundred and sixty-nine** 172 – **a hundred and seventy-two**
184 – **a hundred and eighty-four** 198 – **a hundred and ninety-eight**
200 – **two hundred**

Look!

100 – a hundred (or **one** hundred)
101 – a hundred and one (or **one** hundred and one)
200 – two hundred

6 Listen and say

□ □ children — □ □ canteen
□ □ baby — □ □ moustache
□ □ married — □ □ address
□ □ ninety — □ □ nineteen

7 Listen and say

Plurals

ssss book**s**, date**s**, jacket**s**, passport**s**

zzzz son**s**, brother**s**, daughter**s**

iz hous**es**, watch**es**, box**es**

Language

How many ... have you got?
Have you got ...?

I've got ... I have got ...
I haven't got any.

Are you married?
Are you single?

STUDY

Whose is this?
Whose suitcase is this?

It's	my your his her our their	suitcase.	It's	mine. yours. his. hers. ours. theirs.
It's	Latifa's	suitcase.	It's	Latifa's.

What's it like?	It's blue with a red handle
What's she like?	She's very tall and thin.
What's he like?	He's short and quite fat.
What colour is it?	It's green.
What colour are they?	They're green.

I've got …	I have got …	I haven't got …
He's got …	He has got …	He hasn't got …
She's got …	She has got …	She hasn't got …

Have you got any children?	Yes. I've got two.
Has he got …?	
Has she got …?	
How many … have you got?	I've got four. I haven't got any.

He's got short black hair.

She's got long fair hair.

I'm sorry I'm late.	It doesn't matter.

NEW WORDS

Learn these words.

things

tea
coffee
snacks
fruit juice
a wheel
a handle
a handbag
a suitcase
a ticket
a visa
an address
a pick-up

people

a child
a grandchild
a baby
an officer
the army

adjectives

quite
very

long
short
thin
fat
tall
pretty
married
single

adjectives - colours

black
blue
brown
green
grey
red
white
yellow

blonde (hair)
fair (hair)

the face

eyes
hair
a beard
a moustache

places

a room
a canteen
a village

numbers 101–200

a hundred and one, a hundred and two, … two hundred

UNIT 6 Where is it?

Lesson 1 The second door on the right

1 Listen

Write A B or C.

A

Excuse me. Where's Mrs Brown's classroom?
Go along the corridor and it's the third door on the left.
Thanks very much.

B

Where's room 205?
It's on the second floor.
The second floor? Is there a lift?
It's over there, but it's broken.

C

Good morning.
Good morning. Where's Mr Saeedi's office, please?
It's up the stairs.
On the first floor?
Yes. It's the second door on the right.

2 Write

Write first, second and third in the boxes.

3 Ask and answer

A
Where's … office?

B
Go along the corridor.
It's the first room on the left.
second right.
third

4 Listen and say

Numbers 1st–10th:

1st – **first** 2nd – **second** 3rd – **third** 4th – **fourth** 5th – **fifth**
6th – **sixth** 7th – **seventh** 8th – **eighth** 9th – **ninth** 10th – **tenth**

Numbers 300–1000:

300 – **three hundred** 400 – **four hundred** 500 – **five hundred**
600 – **six hundred** 700 – **seven hundred** 800 – **eight hundred**
900 - **nine hundred** 1000 - **a thousand**

5 Ask and answer

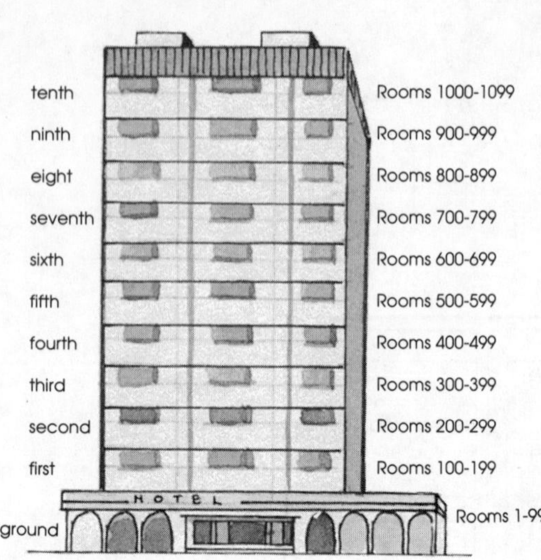

A
Where's room 315?

B
It's on the third floor.

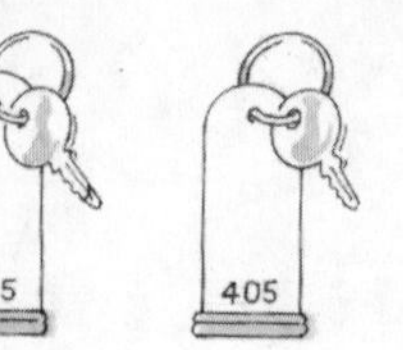

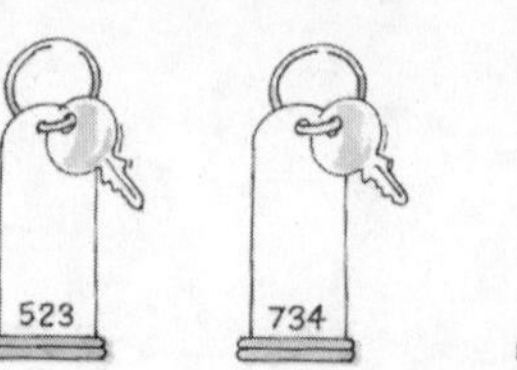

B
Where's room 830?

A
It's on the eighth floor.

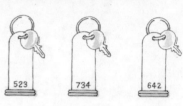

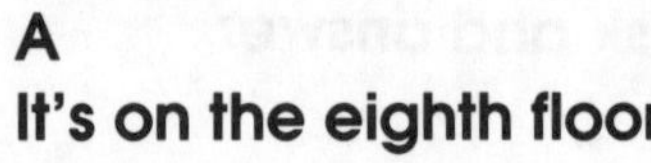

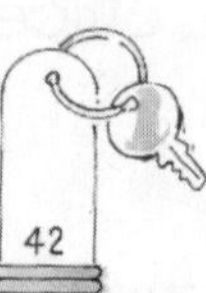

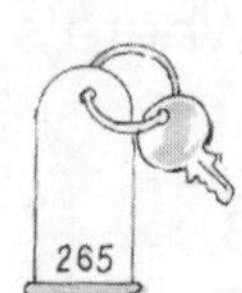

6 Listen

Tick (√) the word you hear.

a) left lift
b) left lift
c) left lift
d) left lift
e) left lift
f) left lift
g) left lift
h) left lift

7 Listen and say

left, red, second, secretary, yes, very;
lift, in, is, this, single, thin, big, women.

Language

on the left
on the right

on the first floor

Is there a ...?
It's broken.
Go along ...

Go!
Stop!
Wait!

Lesson 2 Latifa's village

1 Read

This is a picture of Latifa's village in Oman. It's a very small village. On the left there is a shop and next to the shop there's a small restaurant. On the right there's a mosque and next to it there's a primary school. The village has also got a garage. It's between the school and the restaurant. It's in the middle of the village.

What are they?

a) ______________________ b) ______________________

c) ______________________ d) ______________________

e) ______________________

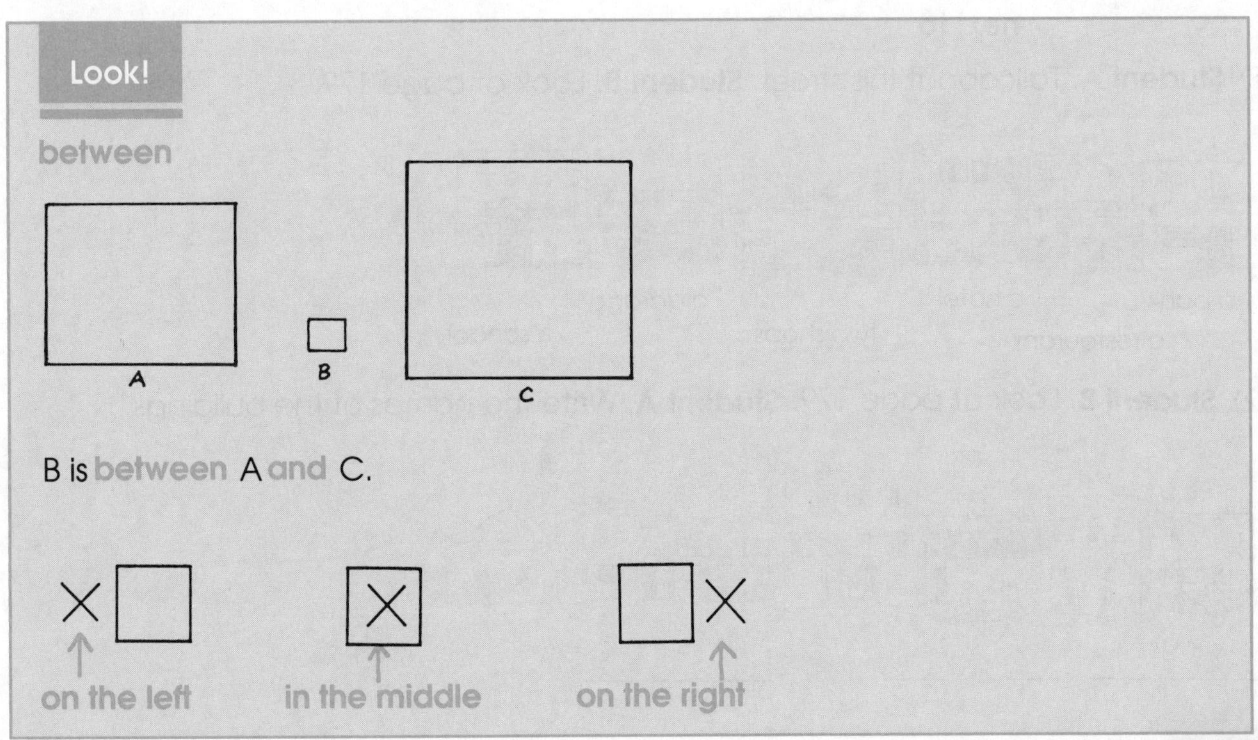

Look!
between
A
B
C
B is between A and C.
on the left
in the middle
on the right

2 Ask and answer

Where's the ...?
Where are the ...?

It's **They're**	**next to ...** **near ...** **between ... and ...** **on the left.** **on the right.** **in the middle.**

a) the mosque?
b) the shops?
c) the school?
d) the restaurant?
e) the garage?

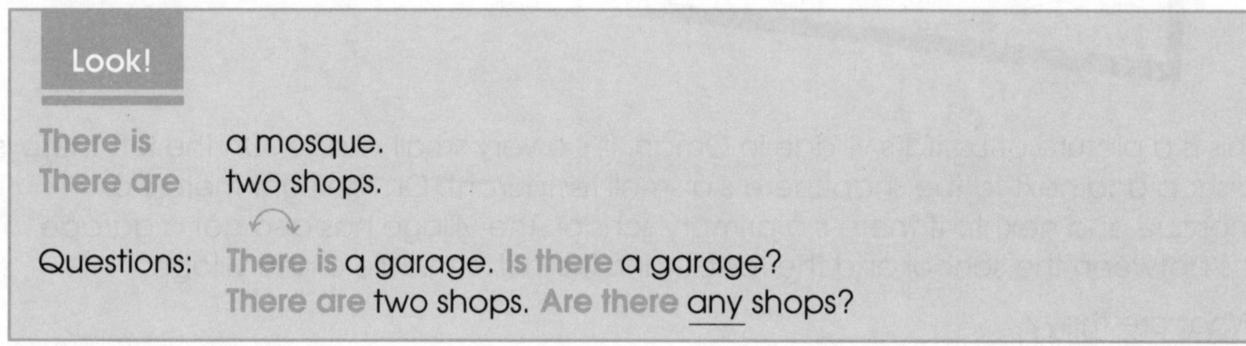

Look!

There is a mosque.
There are two shops.

Questions: There is a garage. Is there a garage?
There are two shops. Are there any shops?

3 Look and say

There's ...
There are ... **between ... and**
on the left/right.
next to

1) **Student A**. Talk about this street. **Student B**. Look at page 179.

2) **Student B**. Look at page 179. **Student A**. Write the names of the buildings.

4 Write

Write **are**, **has**, **quite**, **there**, **a**, **got**, **village**, **primary**, **is ('s)** in the spaces.

A: What's your ________________ like Bashir?

B: It's ________ nice. It's small.

A: Is ________ a school?

B: Yes, there ________ a________ school.

A: Is there ________ mosque?

B: Yes. There ________ two.

A: And ________ it got a hotel?

B: No. But, it's ________ a small restaurant.

5 Read

On the ground floor there's

a kitchen

a sitting room...

a small dining room

and a toilet.

Upstairs there are

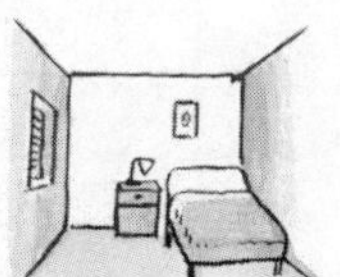

three bedrooms...

and a bathroom.

Match the questions and the answers.

a) How many bedrooms are there?
b) Where's the kitchen?
c) Is there a sitting room upstairs?
d) Where's the bathroom?
e) Is there a dining room on the ground floor?
f) Has it got a dining room upstairs?

1) No, it hasn't.
2) It's on the ground floor.
3) It's upstairs.
4) Yes, there is.
5) There are three.
6) No, there isn't.

6 Listen and say

third, fourth, fifth, sixth, seventh, eighth, ninth, tenth, thin, thanks.

there, they're, their, these, those, this, that, brother, father, mother.

Language

There is
There are
Is there (a) ...?
Are there (any)...?
How many ... are there?

between ... and ...
in the middle

It's got ...
Has it got ...?

Lesson 3 Can I speak to Mrs Roberts?

1 Listen

Write A, B or C.

A

Hello. 567 2343.
Hello. Is Gary Jones there, please?
I'm sorry, he's not here today.
Oh. I'll phone again tomorrow. Goodbye.
Goodbye.

B

Good morning. ITC.
Good morning. Can I speak to Mrs Roberts, please?
Yes. Who is that?
Salem Darwish.
Just a moment please, Mr Darwish.

C

Good afternoon. Middle East Oil Company.
Can I speak to Sam Smith, please?
I'm sorry. Mr Smith is busy.
Oh. Can I speak to his secretary?
Certainly.

Look!

Can I ...

Can I speak to Mr Jones?

Can I have a kilo of oranges?

Can I have a coffee please?

2 Ask and answer

A
Can I speak to … please?

B
I'm sorry. He's out.
She's busy.
not here.
Yes. Just a minute.

a) Mrs Ward (✓)
b) Ahmed (✗)
c) The manager (✗)
d) Mr Saeedi (✓)
e) Selwa (✗)
d) Simon Star (✗)
g) Mr Main's secretary. (✓)

3 Write

Write in these words **can**, **minute**, **sorry**, **morning**, **today**, **speak**, **wife**.

A: Good _________ . Capital English School.

B: Good morning. Can I _________ to Mr Brown please?

A: I'm _________ , Mr Brown is not here _________ .

B: _________ I speak to his _________ ?

A: Yes. Just a _________ please.

Look!

I'll phone again tomorrow. = I will phone again tomorrow.

4 Listen and say

Days of the week

Saturday, Sunday, Monday, Tuesday, Wednesday, Thursday, Friday.

What day is it today? _________

What day is it tomorrow? _________

5 How many?

a) How many days are there in a week? _________

b) How many weeks are there in a year? _________

c) How many days are there in this month? _________

d) How many months are there in a year? _________

6 Listen and say

tomorrow telephone broken today

Write these words in the right place:

between, reception, office, sixteen, manager, second, banana, corridor.

Language

Can I speak to …?
Can I have …?

He's busy.
out.
not here.

Just a minute.

I'll phone again …

today, tomorrow
days of the week

Lesson 4 Peter's classroom

1 Listen

Peter is a new teacher at Capital English School.

Where's Peter's classroom? Put an X.

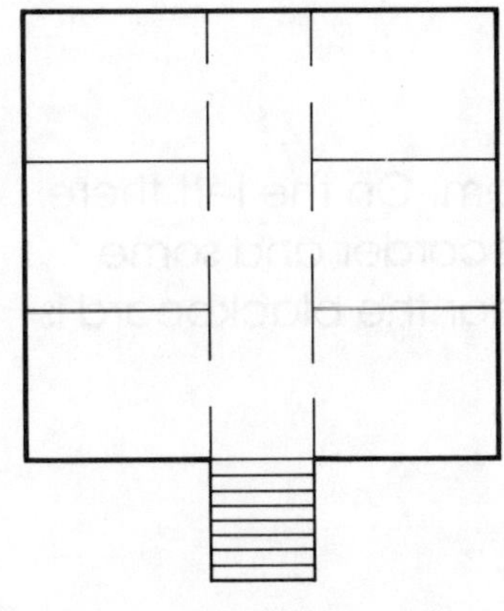

Look!
Go.
Come here.
Come on.
Sit down.

2 Read

Write these words in the list: **desks, table, books, cassette recorder, cupboard, wall, blackboard, windows, teacher's desk, door**.

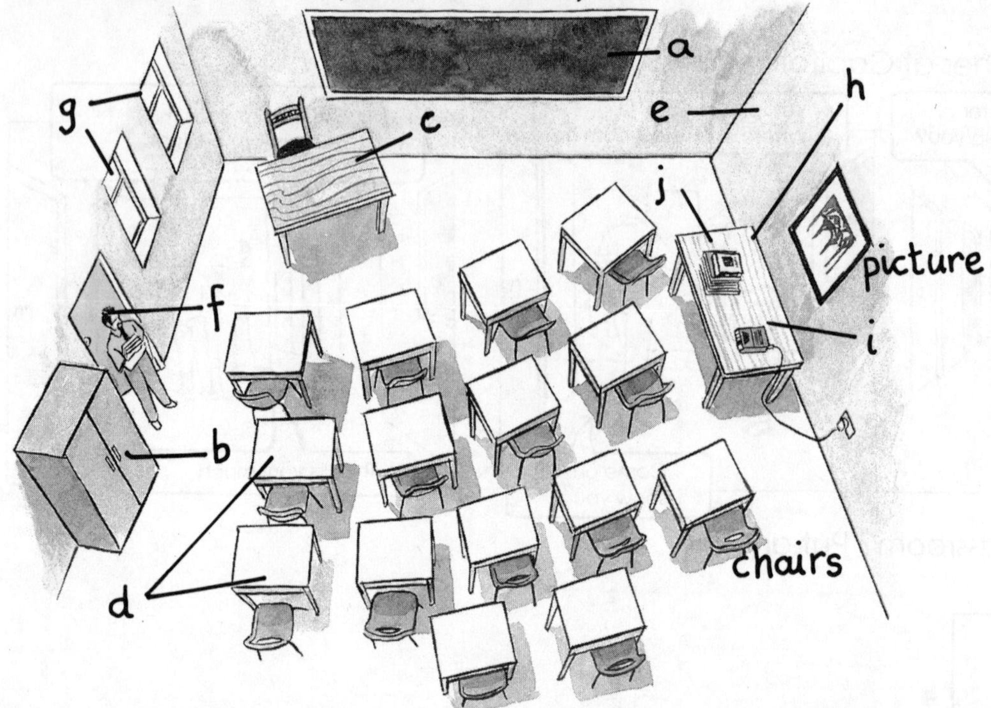

This is Peter's classroom. There are 15 desks and chairs in the room. On the left there are two windows. On the right there's a table with a cassette recorder and some books on it. On the wall in the middle, there's a blackboard. Near the blackboard is the teacher's desk. There's a big cupboard near the door.

a) ____________ f) ____________
b) ____________ g) ____________
c) ____________ h) ____________
d) ____________ i) ____________
e) ____________ j) ____________

Look!

in
There are 15 tables **in** the room.

on
There's a cassette recorder **on** the table.

3 Ask and answer

Where's the ...? **It's ...**
Where are the ...? **They're ...**

a) the cupboard
b) the desks
c) the blackboard
d) the books
e) the teacher's desk
f) the picture
g) the chairs

Look!

Can I	help you?	I'll show you.
	speak to Ahmed?	I'll phone tomorrow.
	have a coffee?	

4 Write

Write **along**, **door**, **I'll**, **far**, **very**, **second**, **help**, **on**, **workshop**.

A: Hello. Can I ________ you?

B: Yes. Where's the ______________________?

A: It's not _________ . ___________ show you.

B: Thanks.

A: Go __________ this corridor. The workshop is _____ the right.

B: Is it the first __________?

A: No. That's the toilet. It's the __________ door.

B: Thank you ________ much.

5 Listen and say

door, or, board, floor, wall, four, fourth.

Sounds and spelling

Listen: **door**, **room**.

6 Listen and say

Silent letters

cu**p**board, stai**r**s, fi**r**st, thi**r**d.

Language

Can I help you?

Come here.
Come on.
Sit down.

I'll show you.

in the room
on the table
on the wall

STUDY

There is a mosque.
There are two shops.

Is there a garage?
Are there any shops?

There's a shop **between** the garage **and** the restaurant.

There's a garage **on the right**.

There's a hotel **on the left**.

There's a school **in the middle of** the village.

There are 15 tables **in** the room.
There's a cassette recorder **on** the table.

Can I ...?
Can I speak to Mrs Roberts, please?

She's busy. / not here. / out.
Yes. Just a minute.

Can I have a kilo of oranges, please? Certainly.
Can I have a coffee, please?

Can I help you?

I'll phone again tomorrow.
I'll show you.

I'll ... = I will ...

Go! Stop! Wait! Come! Sit!

Go along the corridor. Go up the stairs. Go down the stairs.
Come on. Come here. Sit down.

Prepositions
up down along on in between

NEW WORDS

Learn these words.

rooms

a kitchen
a bathroom
a sitting room
an office
a toilet
a bedroom
a classroom
a photocopying room
a computer room
a workshop

things

a table
a door
a window
a picture
a chair
a wall
a desk

time

today
tomorrow
day
week
month

Saturday
Sunday
Monday
Tuesday
Wednesday
Thursday
Friday

places

the stairs
a lift
a restaurant
a coffee shop

adjectives

broken
busy
large

verbs

to go
to stop
to wait
to speak
to help
to have
to show
to phone
to come

numbers

first, second, third, fourth, fifth, sixth, seventh, eighth, ninth, tenth.

one hundred, two hundred, ... a thousand.

______________________ ______________________

______________________ ______________________

______________________ ______________________

______________________ ______________________

______________________ ______________________

______________________ ______________________

REVIEW UNIT C

GRAMMAR

1 Write

That's my book.	That's mine.
your	yours.
his	his.
her	hers.
our	ours.
their	theirs.

Write **my, your, his, her, our, their** in the spaces.

Stop! That's ____________ camera!

This is __________ ice-cream.

That's __________ car.

This is ____________ seat, sir.

That's ____________ pick up.

This is _______________ book.

2 Write

Write sentences like this:

That's mine!

3 Write

I have got …	Have I got …?	It has got …	Has it got …?
You have got …	Have you got …?	We have got …	Have we got …?
He has got …	Has he got …?	They have got …	Have they got …?
She has got …	Has she got …?		

Write **have** or **has**.

a) Our village __________ got two schools.
b) __________ you got any children?
c) She __________ got long black hair.
d) __________ the students got their books?
e) I __________ not got any oranges.
f) __________ your son got a car?
g) We __________ got three sons and two daughters.

4 Write

There is a book on the table.
There are two books on the table.

Write **is** or **are**.

In the classroom there _______ two windows on the right. On the left there _______ a door, and on the wall in the middle there ________ a blackboard. There _______ a table near the blackboard and there _______ five or six books on it. In the middle of the classroom there ______ twelve desks and twelve chairs. On the right, between the windows, there _______ a large cupboard.

Now draw the classroom.

5 Match

Can I help you?
have ...?
speak to ...?

Match the sentences with the pictures.

a) Can I speak to Saeed, please?

b) Can I help you?

c) Can I have a kilo of oranges?

d) 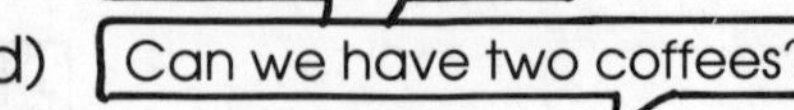

NEW WORDS

6 Rooms

Write the names of the rooms on the picture:

kitchen, bathroom, toilet, sitting room, bedroom, classroom, office, dining room.

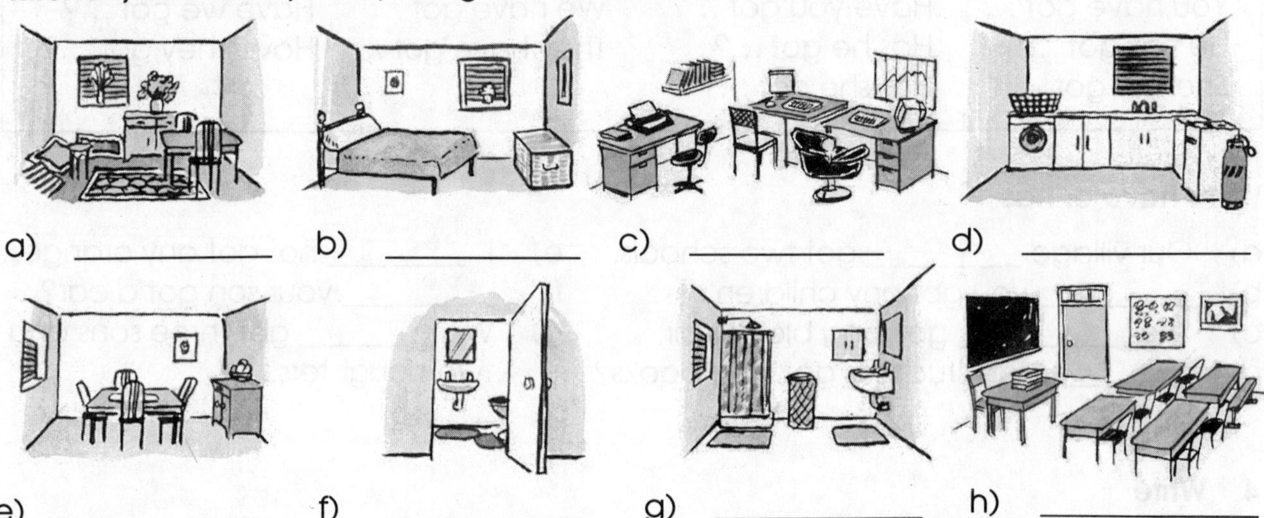

a) ________ b) ________ c) ________ d) ________

e) ________ f) ________ g) ________ h) ________

7 Colours

Write eight sentences about colours.

For example: **My car is red and white.**
Lemons are yellow.

My car Lemons The door	is are	black. white. brown. red. yellow. green. grey. blue.

____
____
____
____
____
____
____
____

8 Numbers

Write the other numbers.

first ______ ______ ______ ______ ______ ______ ______ ______ ______ ______

9 Numbers

Write these numbers:

149	*a hundred and forty-nine*	613	______
175	______	861	______
284	______	999	______
392	______	1000	______

PUNCTUATION

10 Write

Put in punctuation and capital letters.

a) wheres mrs browns classroom ______

b) hes got two children ______

c) im simon stars secretary ______

d) thats latifas ______

e) can i speak to john main please ______

f) ill phone again on sunday ______

g) the managers office is on the left ______

h) ive got brown eyes and grey hair ______

SPELLING

11 Look

Find 12 spelling mistakes.

My name's Suhair. I'm tharty-two yars old and I'm from Tanta in Egypt. I'm a teacher in a pirmary school. I'm maried and I've got tow childrn, a boy and a gairl. My husband is a clerk in a bank. Our flat is neer the centre of Tanta. It's got two bedroms, a siting room, a kitchen and a bahtroom. It's on the forth floor.

READ AND WRITE

12 Read

Read about Damascus Street.

I live in in a small street in Cairo. It's called Damascus Street. We've got three shops, two hotels, a mosque, a café and a restaurant in our street. There is also a small garage. The garage is on the left, on the corner. It's called Hassan's Garage. Hassan's the owner. Next to the garage is a small hotel, the First Class Hotel. It's cheap, but it's not very nice. After that, there's our building. We are between the hotel and a café. There are always many people at the café. It's very busy. Next to the café there's a shop. The owner is Mustapha. He's a friend of mine. On the right of the street there's a restaurant and a hotel – the Momtaz Hotel. It has got a large entrance. Next to the hotel there are two small shops. The first is a bakery and the second has got fruit and vegetables. After that, at the end of the street, there's a big mosque.

Now complete the plan. Write: **shop**, **bakery**, **mosque**, **Momtaz Hotel**, **restaurant**, **First Class Hotel**, **Hassan's Garage**.

mosque
shop
café
house
hotel
garage
shop
bakery
hotel
restaurant

13 Write

Write in the missing words.

Charles – 30
engineer – oil company – Dubai
married – one son

Charles has ____________ blue eyes __________ short fair ________ . He's about 30 ______ old. He's got ______ moustache, but he _________ got a beard. He's ______ and quite thin. He's _______ engineer _________ an oil company in Dubai. He's ______ and he's got a son.

Aisha – 29
doctor – hospital – Cairo
single

My sister, Aisha, has got brown _____ and long black ______ . She's ______ and she's quite fat. ______ 's 29 years _______ . She's _______ doctor in a hospital ______ Cairo. She's not married.

14 Write

Write about these two people:

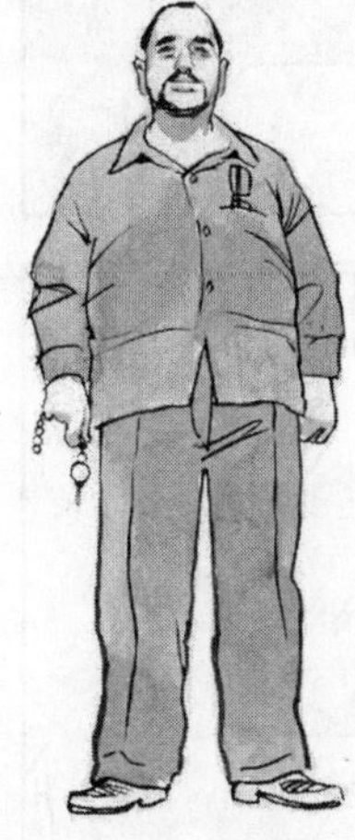

Ali – 36
taxi driver – Jeddah
married – eight children

Susan – 43
secretary – ITC – Amman
married – two children

Good morning, Khalid. What's the problem?
My grandfather. He's not in the hotel.

Not in the hotel? Where is he?
I don't know.

Let's look in the street.
OK. Maybe he's there.

He's not here.
Look. I'll ask that policeman.

Your grandfather? What's he like?
He's small and he's got a grey beard.

How old is he?
HOTEL
He's about 65.

UNDERGROUND

I'll phone the hotel.
TELEPHONE

Forum Hotel. Good Morning.

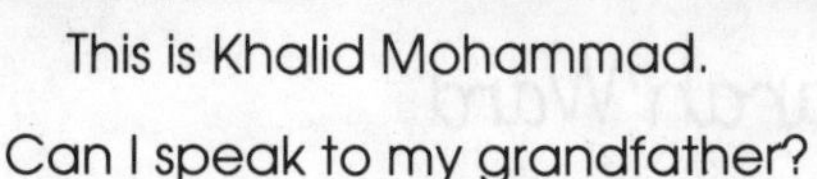
This is Khalid Mohammad.
Can I speak to my grandfather?

I'm sorry, Mr Mohammad,
your grandfather's not here.

Let's look in
the park.
TELEPHONE

Look! He's there!

Grandfather!
Hello. What a
beautiful day!

WORKBOOK

Unit 1 Meeting People

Lesson 1 **Hello!** Hello

1 Dictation

Listen and write the names.

A ___ B _____ S _____ Y _______

G _____ K _____ T ___ B _____

S _____ W ____ S _____ D _______

2 Read and match

Tom Brown
Sarah Ward
John Main
Sam Smith
Jane Clark
Mary Brown
Ann Barry

John Main *Tom Brown* *Sam Smith*

Mary Brown *Anne Barry*

Jane Clark *Sarah Ward*

3 Read and write

Read the sentences.

apostrophe

Hello, I'm Ann Jones. *Hello, Mrs Jones, I'm Selwa Yasser.*

capital letters comma full stop

John Mail Saeed Darwish

Write two more sentences.

Hello, I'm ____________________

Hello, ____________________

4 Write

Write the names in the lists:

Sarah, Tom, Gary, Ann, John, Sam, Mary, Jane.

Sarah

Tom

5 Punctuation (', . ?) and capital letters

Write these sentences with punctuation and capital letters.

a) im gary kent ______

b) how are you ______

c) fine thanks ______

d) hello mrs long ______

Lesson 2 My name's Bond

1 Group work

Write the names of your group in the table. Ask and answer like this:

What's your name please? **My name's Tawfiq, T A W F I Q.**

GROUP ____.

1 ______

2 ______

3 ______

4 ______

5 ______

2 Write

Hello, ______ Sarah Ward.
Hello Mrs ______. How ______?
______, ______ you.

3 Spelling

Match the words.

Hello.	Helo, Heloo, Hallo, Heelo, Hello
all right	all right, alrght, alrihgt, allright, al right
name	nam, naim, name, nema, naem
please	plis, pleas, pleese, please, plaese
fine	fayn, fain, fine, fane, fien
sorry	sory, sarry, sorry, sorri, sary

4 Punctuation (. ? ',) and capital letters

Write these sentences with punctuation and capital letters.

a) my names mohammad yousef

______

b) how are you

______

c) im john main

______

d) im fine thank you

______

e) whats your name

______

f) are you mrs brown

______

5 Write

Answer the question.

My name's Mohammad Yousef. What's your name?

____

Lesson 3 This is Ahmed

1 Write

Write in the missing words.

1) Hello, Jassim. How ______ ______?
Hello, Bob. I'm ______, ______.
2) ______ ______ my friend Khalid.
3) How ______ ______ ______?
______ ______ meet you.

Look!

John Main

first name ↗ ↖ family name

Hello, John.
Hello, Mr Main.

2 Match

Match the answers, with the questions.

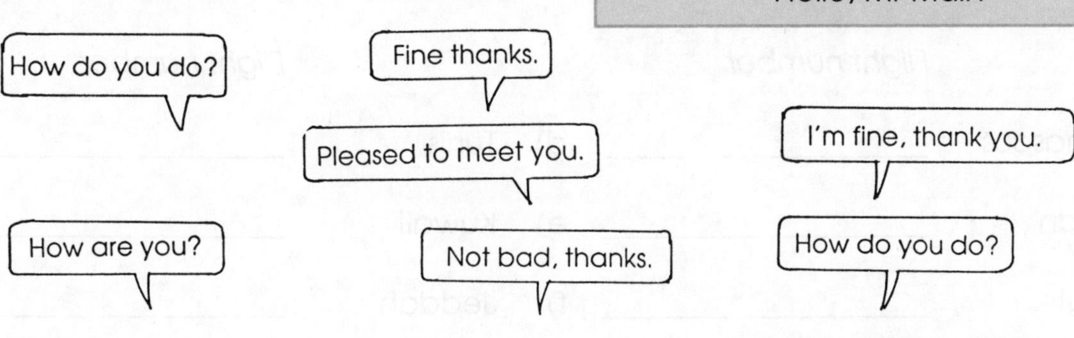

How do you do?
Fine thanks.
Pleased to meet you.
I'm fine, thank you.
How are you?
Not bad, thanks.
How do you do?

3 Write

Make two lists from these names.

First name | *Family name*

John | Main

4 Listen and write

Listen to the flight numbers and write them down.

	Flight number		*Flight number*
a) Damascus		d) Tunis	
b) Aswan		e) Kuwait	
c) Beirut		f) Jeddah	

5 Listen and write

Write A, B or C below the pictures.

Now write: **Mrs Brown**! **Mrs Brown**? and **Mrs Brown**.

6 Write

Put the words in the right order.

a) friend / my / is / this ______

b) do / how / you / do? ______

c) to / pleased / you / meet ______

d) name / is / your / what? ______

e) name / Khalid / is / my ______

Lesson 4 Good morning

1 Read and write

Good ______, Khalifa. How ______?
I'm ______ thank you. ______?
______

2 Spelling

Match the words.

friend	frend, frind, freind, friend, firind
pleased	peleased, pleased, plesed, pleesed, pleazed
morning	mrning, mornig, mornning, morning, mourning
afternoon	afternon, afternoon, aftrnoon, aftrenoon, afeternoon
evening	evening, evning, ivening, evenig, eevning
night	night, nihgt, nigth, naight, nght

3 Write

Write the answer.

a) Good morning. ____________________

b) How are you? ____________________

c) How do you do? ____________________

d) What's your name? ____________________

e) Are you Mr Darwish? ____________________

4 Group work

Write down the names and telephone numbers of the people in your group.

What's your name?
What's your telephone number?

Example: **Saeed – 763928**

Group ______

a) ____________________

b) ____________________

c) ____________________

d) ____________________

e) ____________________

5 Numbers

Write the numbers.

0 ______, 1 ______, 2 ______,

3 ______, 4 ______, 5 ______,

6 ______, 7 ______, 8 ______,

9 ______, 10 ______.

6 Write

Write **is ('s), am ('m)** or **are** in the spaces.

a) What ______ your name?

b) How ______ you?

c) I ______ pleased to meet you.

d) This ______ my friend, Khalid.

e) I ______ fine, thank you.

f) ______ you Mrs Brown?

7 Crossword

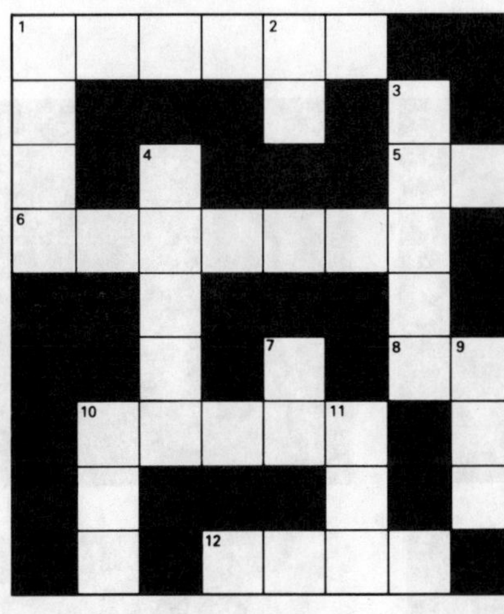

Across →

1 This is my ..., Ahmed.
5 My name ... Selwa.
6 morning, afternoon, ..., night
8 Pleased ... meet you.
10 "Mr Main?"
"No, I'm Mr Brown."
"Oh, I'm ..."
12 two, three ..., five

Down ↓

1 "How are you?" "I'm ..., thank you."
2 Yes and ...
3 "I'm sorry!" "That's all ..."
4 Hi!
7 "I'm Tom Brown." "Hello ... Brown."
9 ... two, three, four
10 four, five ... seven
11 Are ... Mrs Brown?

Unit 2 Family and Friends

Lesson 1 Who's that?

1 Write

Write the words in the spaces.

2 Ask and answer

Who's that?

That's ....
I don't know.

3 Spelling

Match the words.

mother	mother, mothr, mather, mothre, moter
brother	brather, brother, brothre, brohter, berother
daughter	dautgher, daugther, doghter, daghter, daughter
grandfather	granfarther, granfather, grandfther, grandfather, grandfathr
sister	siseter, sisster, sester, saster, sister,
nice	nice, naice, niyc, niec, neic
handsome	hansome, hamsome, handsom, hendsome, handsome,

4 Match

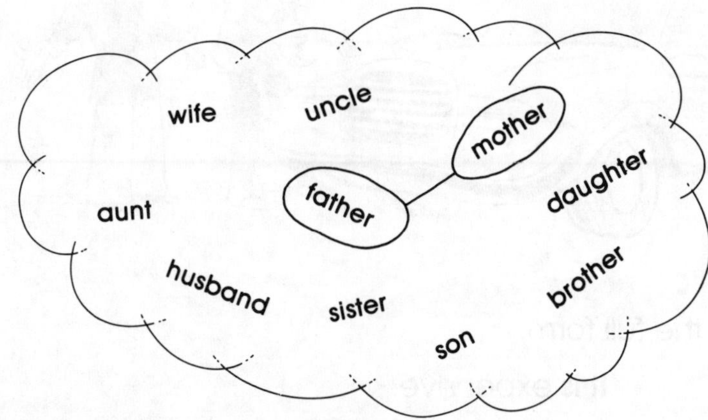

5 Punctuation (', . ?) and capital letters

Write these sentences with punctuation and capital letters.

a) his names ahmed ______________________

b) im tom brown ______________________

c) this is my wife sarah ______________________

d) alis very handsome ______________________

e) my names tawfiq ______________________

f) whats her name ______________________

6 Write

Write **my, your, his** and **her** in the dialogue.

A: Good morning. *B:* Good morning.

A: What's _______ name please? *B:* _______ name's Tom Brown.

A: Is this _______ wife, Mr Brown? *B:* Yes. _______ name's Mary.

A: Mary Brown? *B:* Yes. That's right.

A: And who's this? *B:* That's _______ son. _______ name's Robert.

Lesson 2 **Good Luck Hotel**

1 Write

Write in the words.

It's new. It's cheap.
No. It's ________ and
it's ________.

2 Write

Write these sentences in the full form.

Example: **It's** expensive. **It is** expensive.

a) I'm seven and a half. ________
b) My sister's very nice. ________
c) His name's Tom. ________
d) I'm pleased to meet you. ________
e) Who's that? ________
f) What's your name? ________

3 Spelling

Write in the missing vowels: **a**, **e**, **i**, **o**, **u**.

a) c h __ __ p
b) __ x p __ n s __ v __
c) n __ m __
d) p l __ __ s __ d
e) y __ __ n g
f) h __ t __ l
g) b r __ t h __ r

4 Numbers

Write these numbers:

11 ____________________

12 ____________________

13 ____________________

14 ____________________

15 ____________________

5 Ask and answer

How old?

How old is ...? **He's ...**
She's ...

Student A	
Bashir	4
Salwa	13
Mahmoud	
Khadija	9 1/2
Aisha	
Habiba	
Tawfiq	
Hamoud	11
Nora	15
Yasser	

Student B	
Bashir	
Salwa	
Mahmoud	10
Khadija	
Aisha	5
Habiba	6 1/2
Tawfiq	14
Hamoud	
Nora	
Yasser	12

How old are you? ____________________

6 Write

Write **I**, **you**, **he**, **she**, **it** in the spaces.

a) Hello. How are __________?

b) This is my daughter. _________ is ten years old.

c) My name's Khalid. _________ am pleased to meet you.

d) That is the Good Luck Hotel. _________ is cheap.

e) "Are ______ Tom Brown?"
"Yes, that's right."

f) This is my uncle. __________ is very nice.

Lesson 3 Where are you from?

1 Countries

Write in the vowels **a, e, i, o, u**.

a) S___ ___d___ ___r___b___ ___

b) B___hr___ ___n

c) L___b___n___n

d) ___lg___r___ ___

e) K___w___ ___t

f) ___m___r___c___

2 Questions

Put the words in order.

a) you / from / are / where ?

Where ______________________

b) you / are / how ?

____

c) old / you / how / are ?

____

d) Kuwait / you / are / from ?

____

e) please / what / name / is / your ?

____

3 Match

Match the questions with the answers.

a)	Where are you from?	I'm 18.
b)	How are you?	Yes, from London.
c)	Are you from England?	Not bad, thanks.
d)	How old are you?	From Cairo.

4 Write

Write **who, what**, or **where** in the dialogue.

A: ________'s that?
B: That's my friend, Salim.

A: Oh. ________'s he from?
B: From Tanta.

A: Tanta? ____________'s that?
B: In Egypt.

A: And ________'s that?
B: That's his hotel.

5 Read

Match the people with the countries. Write the names on the map.

1) My name's Latifa Al-Rashid. I'm from Sur in Oman.
2) I'm Mohammad. I'm from Tunisia.
3) My name's Ahmed Mansour. I'm from Muharraq in Bahrain.
4) I'm Samia. I'm from Rabat in Morocco.
5) My name's Fahad. I'm from Aswan in Egypt.

Latifa

Mohammad

Ahmed

Samia

Fahad

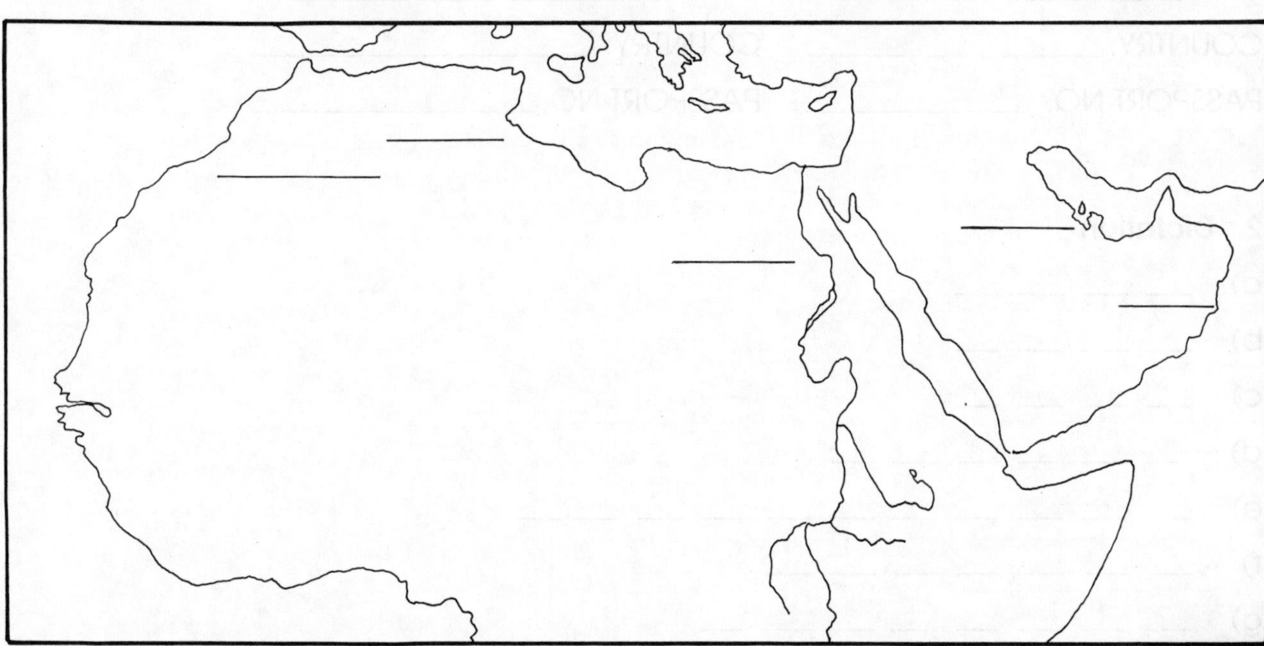

6 Write

Read this sentence again:

My name's Latifa Al-Rashid. I'm from Sur in Oman.

Now write about yourself.

What's your name?
Where are you from?

____

____

Lesson 4 Welcome!

1 Ask and answer

What's your name, please?
How do you spell that?
Where are you from?
What's your passport number?

You	*Your partner*
NAME: ________________	NAME: ________________
CITY: ________________	CITY: ________________
COUNTRY: ________________	COUNTRY: ________________
PASSPORT NO. ________________	PASSPORT NO. ________________

2 Dictation

a) __ __ __ __

b) __ __ __ __

c) __ __ __ __

d) __ __ __ __ __ __

e) __ __ __ __ __ __ __ __ __ __ __

f) __ __ __ __ __ __ __

g) __ __ __ __ __ __ __ __

3 Spelling

Match the words.

welcome	wellcom, wellcome, wilcome, welcome, willcom
police	polis, bleas, police, polise, plice
passport	pasport, passport, paseport, pusporet, bassport
where	wher, were, wheer, where, ware
spell	spel, spell, espell, speel, speil
England	Engeland, Englnd, Engaland, Ingland, England

4 Look

Find the word that is different.

a) mother, sister, wife, uncle, daughter, aunt.
b) father, son, friend, cousin, sister, grandmother.
c) handsome, tall, nice, hotel, good, small, bad.
d) nineteen, eight, twelve, eleven, number, four, thirteen.
e) it, my, you, I, he, she.

5 Punctuation (', . ?) and capital letters

Write these sentences with capital letters and punctuation.

a) hassan is from egypt ______________________________
b) mrs brown is from england ______________________________
c) sousse is in tunisia ______________________________
d) fawzia is from rabat in morocco ______________________
e) sam smith is from dallas in texas ______________________
f) wheres tom brown from ______________________________

6 Write

Write the words **in, from, not, welcome, are, where, am ('m), is ('s), you** in the spaces.

A: What _____ your name please?
B: Sam Smith.

A: _____ to Abu Dhabi, Mr Smith.
B: Thanks.

A: How do _____ spell your family name?
B: S-M-I-T-H

A: _____ are you _____?
B: I _____ from the United States of America.

A: _____ you from New York?
B: No, I'm _____. I'm from Dallas _____ Texas.

7 Crossword

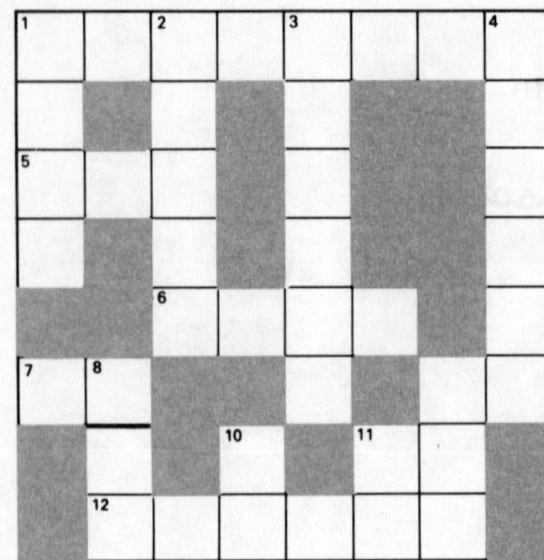

Across →

1 

5 This is my aunt. ... is from Bahrain.
6 GOOD ... HOTEL
7 Hello!
9 This is my friend, Ahmed. ... is from Saudi Arabia.
11 "Who's that. He's handsome."
"Thank you. That's ...!"
12 Father and ...

Down ↓

1 ... and pull.
2 How do you ...your name?
3 

4 seven and five = ?
8 Hello. ... ... Tom Brown. (1, 2)
9 This is my daughter. ... name is Alia.
10 This is my car. ... is new.
11 Excuse ... Where are you from?

Unit 3 Jobs and Nationalities

Lesson 1 He's a mechanic

1 Read

This is my husband, Saeed. He's a policeman.

This is my daughter. She's a student.

My name's Fahd. I'm from Sharjah in the United Arab Emirates.

I'm a doctor. This is my new car. It's a Datsun.

2 Write

My name's Nora. I'm from Latakia in Syria. I'm a secretary.

What about you?

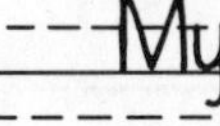

3 Spelling

Match the words:

teacher	techer, teechr, teacher, teachre, teachr
student	studant, studient, student, sudent, studetn
doctor	dactor, doctor, docter, dactr, doceter,
driver	drivr, draiver, drivier, drever, driver
policeman	pliceman, boliceman, poleesman, poliseman, policeman
nurse	nurse, narse, nairse, nurce, nares,
woman	wimin, woeman, woman, wommen, women
girl	garl, girl, girel, gairl, gril

4 Write

Write sentences like this:

She's a nurse. **No, she isn't a nurse. She's a doctor.**

a)

He's a mechanic. No, ____________________. He's ____________________

b)

You're a taxi driver. No, ____________________. I'm ____________________

c)

She's a student. No, ______________________. She's ______________________

d)

I'm a policeman. No, ______________________. You're ______________________

5 Write

Write the words **your**, **a**, **from**, **are** in the spaces.

A: Where __________ you from?

B: I'm __________ Dammam in Saudi Arabia.

A: What's __________ job?

B: I'm __________ driver in ARAMCO.

6 Write

Write the words **a**, **isn't**, **her**, **aunt**, **who**, **is** in the spaces.

A: _____'s that?

B: That's my _______

A: What's _____ name?

B: Fawzia.

A: _____ she a teacher?

B: No, she _____. She's _____ secretary.

7 Punctuation ('. . ?) and capital letters.

Write these sentences with punctuation and capital letters:

a) are you a doctor ______

b) whats your job ______

c) i dont have a job ______

d) he isnt a mechanic ______

e) youre not a nurse ______

f) is she a secretary ______

g) im not a driver ______

Hi. I'm a basketball player.

Lesson 2 These are my brothers

1 Write

Write sentences like this.

This is	my	friend.
These are		friends.

Choose from these words: **cousin/cousins, son/sons, grandfather, aunt/aunts, daughter/daughters, uncle/uncles**.

______ ______

______ ______

2 Spelling

Write **a**, **e**, **i**, **o**, **u** in these words:

a) t _ _ ch _ r

b) p _ l _ t

c) th _ s _

d) m _ ch _ n _ c

e) st _ d _ nt

f) fr _ _ nd

g) s _ cr _ t _ ry

h) sch _ _ l

3 Write

Write **is** or **are** in the spaces.

a) This ______ my car.

b) Mariam ______ a teacher at Capital English School.

c) These ______ my friends.

d) Mr and Mrs Brown ______ from England.

e) He ______ a driver for ARAMCO.

f) They ______ mechanics.

4 Write

Write sentences. Use the table.

He's She's	a student.
They're	students.

a)

He's a teacher.

b)

______

c) ______

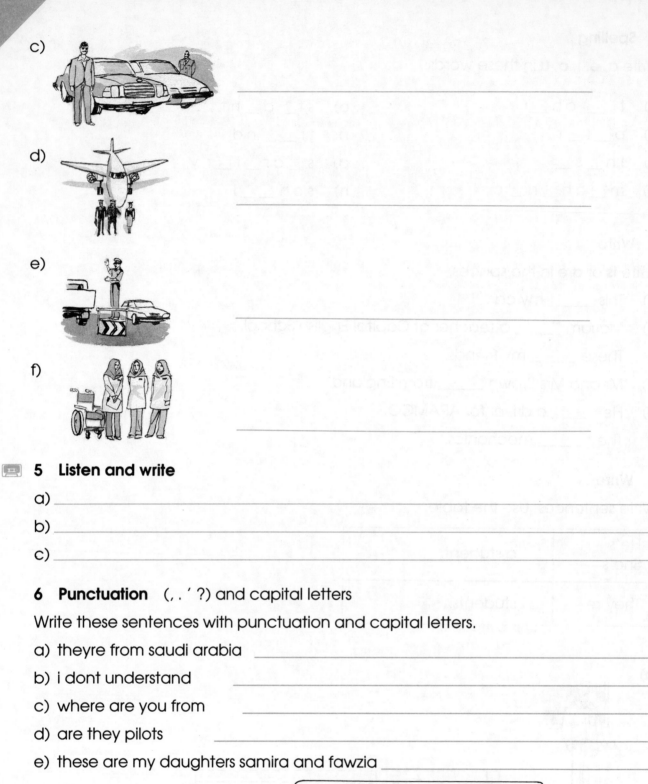

d) ______

e) ______

f) ______

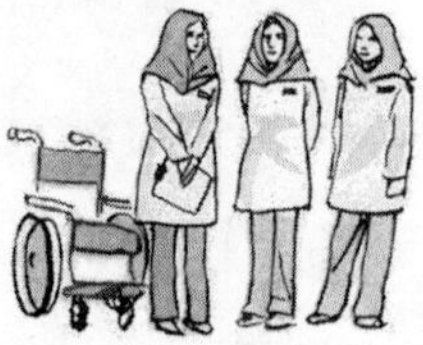

5 Listen and write

a) ______

b) ______

c) ______

6 Punctuation (, . ' ?) and capital letters

Write these sentences with punctuation and capital letters.

a) theyre from saudi arabia ______

b) i dont understand ______

c) where are you from ______

d) are they pilots ______

e) these are my daughters samira and fawzia ______

I'm sorry. I don't understand.

Lesson 3 Are you English?

1 Read and write

My friend is a doctor. His name is Abdul Qader and he is 25 years old. He is from Aswan in Egypt, but he's not Egyptian. He's Sudanese.

My cousin is from Manama in Bahrain. Her name is Suhair and she is Bahraini. She is a teacher in a secondary school. She is 29.

Tawfiq is Palestinian. He's 22 years old and he is a mechanic in a garage. He is from Nablus.

Fawzia is 18 years old and she is from Tanta in Egypt. She is Egyptian. She is a secretary in a bank.

Name	*Age*	*Job*	*Nationality*
Abdul Qader	25	a doctor	Sudanese
Suhair			
Tawfiq			
Fawzia			

Look!

and	His name is Abdul Qader. He is 25 years old. His name is Abdul Qader **and** he is 25 years old.
but	He is from Aswan in Egypt. He is not Egyptian. He is from Aswan in Egypt, **but** he is not Egyptian.

2 Write

Join the sentences with **and**.

a) Suhair is a teacher in a secondary school. She is 29 years old.

____

____

b) My husband is from Alexandria in Egypt. He is a secretary in a bank.

____

____

c) Ali and Lutfi are from Jeddah. They are students.

____

____

3 Listen

Complete the form.

NAME: ______________
CITY: ______________
COUNTRY: ______________
NATIONALITY: ______________

4 Write

Write **I**, **you**, **he**, **she**, **it**, **we**, **they** in the spaces.

a) My friend, Yousef, is from Aleppo. _____ is Syrian.

b) This is my cousin, Samira. ______ is Tunisian.

c) My husband and I are from Algiers. ______ are Algerian.

d) This is my car. ______ is a Toyota.

e) These are my friends, Bahir and Jamal. ______ are students.

f) My name's Ali. _____ am Bahraini.

g) "Are ______ Egyptian?"
"Yes. I'm from Cairo."

5 Ask and answer

Choose a country and a nationality

A	B
Where are you from?	**I'm from …**
Are you …?	**Yes, I am.**
	No, I'm not. I'm …

6 Write

Write the words **am**, **in**, **a**, **from**, **is**, **is** in the spaces.

My name ______ Khalifa. I ______ 26 years old. I am ______ Gabes ______ Tunisia.
I am ______ taxi-driver. My nationality ______ Tunisian.

Now write a paragraph about yourself.

7 **Word puzzle**

Find 12 more nationalities.

```
H S U D A N E S E F
O I R A Q I B A L R
E L E B A N E S E E
M D G O T A L Y U N
I U Y X A T O R I C
R T P B R I T I S H
A C T U I M J A L K
T H I D O M A N I R
I B A L G E R I A N
E O N S A U D I K V
```

Lesson 4 Where are we?

1 **Match**

Match with the pictures.

We're very sorry.

So am I.

Are we late?

Yes, you are!

That's all right.

I'm cold.

2 Write

Use the table.

I am	We are
You are	You are
He is She is It is	They are

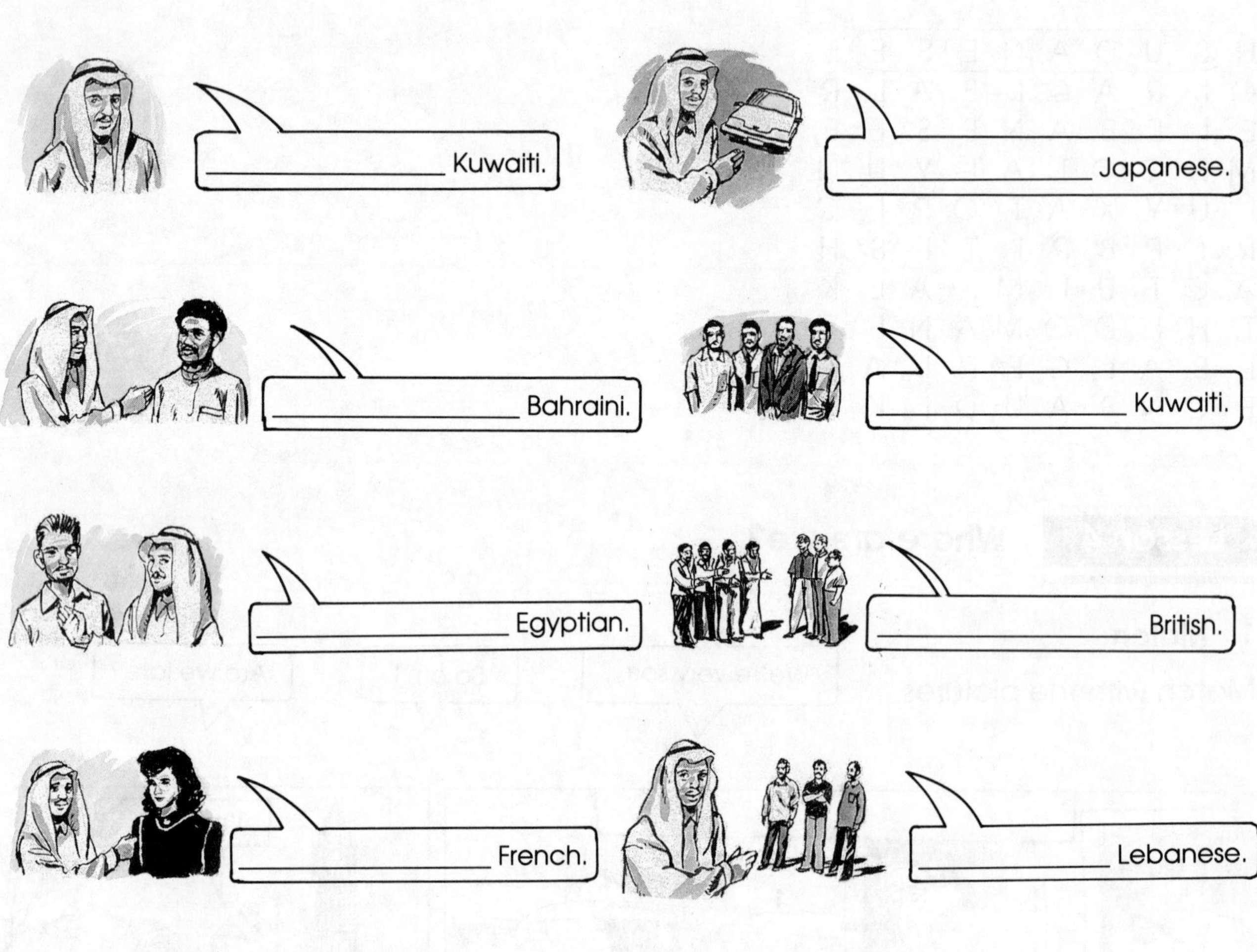

3 Numbers

Write these numbers:

21 ____________________ 26 ____________________

22 ____________________ 27 ____________________

23 ____________________ 28 ____________________

24 ____________________ 29 ____________________

25 ____________________ 30 ____________________

4 Listen and draw

Follow the numbers.

1 2 3 4 5 6 7

8 9 10 11 12 13 14

15 16 17 18 19 20 21

22 23 24 25 26 27 28

It's a ____________________

5 Write

Find the jobs.

a) c h a t r e e ____________

b) n a i h c c e m ____________

c) l o p i t ____________

d) s r e n u ____________

e) o d t r o c ____________

f) r i d e v r ____________

g) n a p i l m o c e ____________

6 Punctuation (, . '?)

Write these sentences with punctuation and capital letters:

my names abdul rahim im from abu dhabi im 26 years old and im a clerk

____

____

7 Crossword

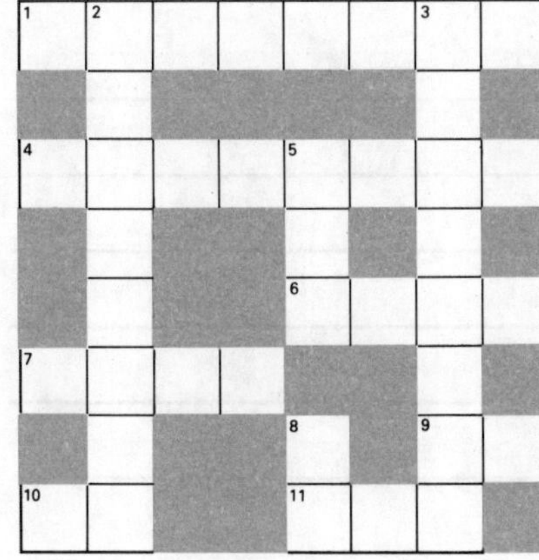

Across →

1

4 She's from Manama. She's …

6

7 Sharjah is … Dubai.

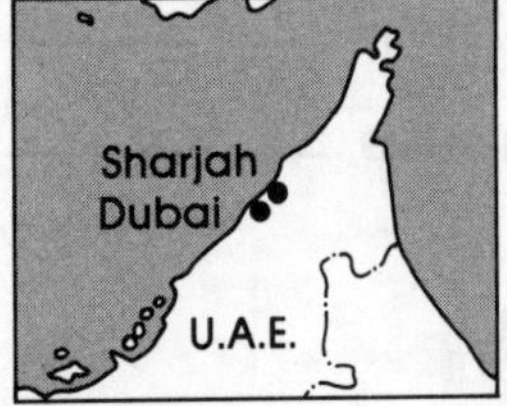

9 "I … late."

10 My sister … a nurse.

11 Six and four.

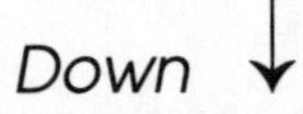

Down ↓

2 They are …

3 They are from Sousse. They are …

5 We are cold … hungry.

8 Welcome to my hotel. … is very good.

Unit 4 In the City

Lesson 1 What's that?

1 Write

Look!

It's a bank. It's beautiful.
It's a beautiful bank.

a) It's a car. It's new. It's a ____________________

b) It's a palace. It's big. ____________________

c) It's a building. It's tall. ____________________

d) It's a hotel. It's cheap. ____________________

e) It's a school. It's very good. ____________________

2 Write

Write sentences from the words like the examples below.

old / car It's an old car.

new / camera It's a new camera.

a) tall / building ____________________

b) beautiful / palace ____________________

c) expensive / car ____________________

d) nice / hotel ____________________

e) new / bank ____________________

f) old / house ____________________

3 Spelling

Match the words.

building *bilding, biulding, building, buildig, buliding*
palace *place, balace, palase, pelace, palace*
hotel *hotal, hotle, hotel, otel, hottel*
school *shool, shcool, schol, sekool, school*
bank *bank, banek, bunk, pank, banc*
hospital *hospitl, hospitle, haspital, hopsital, hospital*
house *hous, hause, house, huse, howse*

4 Write

It's a man.
It isn't a man.
It's a tree.

a) 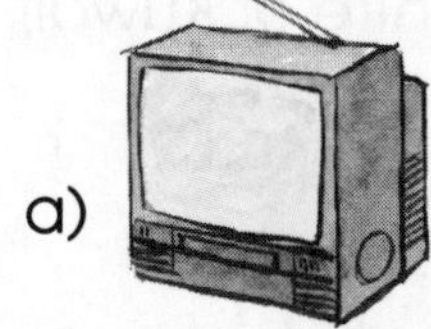

"It's a camera." "It isn't ______ ______. It's ______."

b) 

"It's a watch." "It isn't ______ ______. It's ______."

c) 

"It's a car." ______. ______.

d) 

"It's a bag." ______. ______.

e)

"It's a boy." ______. ______.

f)  

"It's a sandwich." ______. ______.

5 Write

Complete the signs.

(a) R _ C _ P T _ _ N

(b) L _ F T

(c) T _ L _ P H _ N _

(d) T _ _ L _ T S

(e) P _ S H

(f) P _ L L

(g) _ X C H _ N G _ $ £

(h) N _ S M _ K _ N G

(i) _ M M _ G R _ T _ _ N

6 Read and match

1) This is a new hotel. It's the Diplomat Hotel in Cairo. It's near the River Nile.

2) The Capital English School is in Bahrain. It is a small school and it is in the centre of the city.

3) This is my hotel – the Good Luck Hotel. It's a nice hotel. It isn't very big, but it's cheap and it's clean.

4) The Arabian Gulf Bank is a very big bank. It is near the park in the centre of Kuwait City.

A

C

B

D

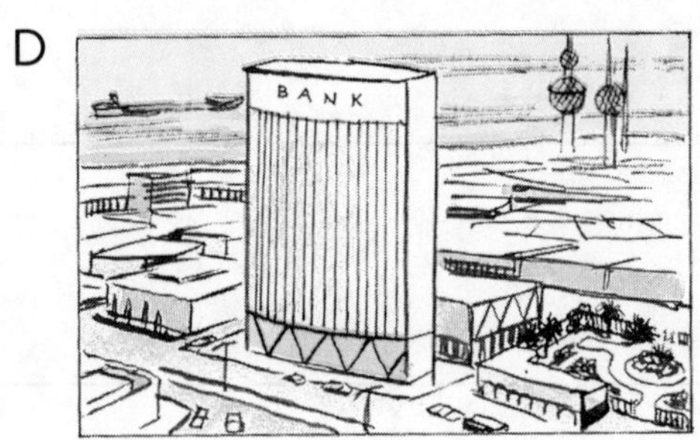

Lesson 2 Is it far?

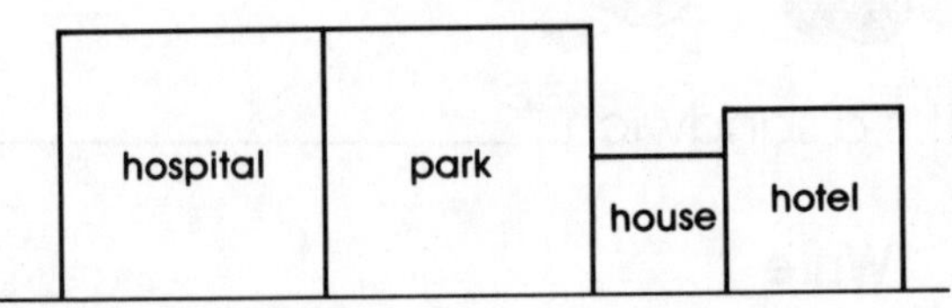

1 Write

Use the table to write sentences.

The mosque	is near	the market.
The school		the bus station.

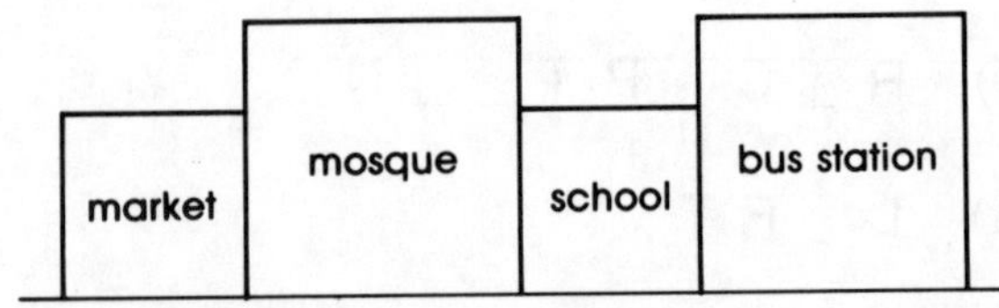

a) The mosque is near the school.

b) __________

c) __________

d) __________

e) __________

2 Questions

Put the words in order.

a) hospital / is / where / the ? __________

b) nationality / what / your / is ? __________

c) old / are / you / how ? __________

d) number / is / your / what / telephone ? __________

e) do / that / spell / you / how ? __________

f) books / are / where / my ? __________

3 Write

Write **a**, **an**, **the**, **(-)** in the spaces.

a) It's _____ expensive camera.

b) They're _____ old houses.

c) He's _____ big man.

d) She's _____ old woman.

e) It's _____ Capital English School.

f) It's _____ tall building.

g) It's _____ Tower of London.

h) They're _____ expensive hotels.

4 Write

Write these sentences in the right order:

a) The Assabeel Hotel.

b) Pardon?

c) No, not far. It's about a kilometre.

d) Excuse me, where's the Assabeel Hotel?

e) It's near the bus station.

f) Is it far?

____

____

____

____

____

____

5 Write

Write **in, from, to** in the spaces.

a) Mariam is _____ Algiers. She's Algerian.

b) The mosque is next _____ the park.

c) We're _____ Aleppo _____ Syria.

d) The airport is not far _____ the city.

e) The Taj Mahal is _____ India.

6 Punctuation (' , . ?) and capital letters

> **Look!**
>
> It's a bank.
> It's the Bank of Bahrain.

Write out these sentences with punctuation and capital letters.

a) whats that ______________________________

b) its my new car ______________________________

c) thats the sheraton hotel ______________________________

d) is that the bank of oman ______________________________

e) were near the school ______________________________

Excuse me, where's the airport?
Pardon?

Lesson 3 The market

1 Write

This apple	is	sweet good. bad. nice. cheap. expensive.
These oranges	are	

a) dates / sweet These ______________________

b) watermelon / bad This ______________________

c) lemons / cheap ______________________

d) bananas / good ______________________

e) apple / nice ______________________

f) oranges / expensive ______________________

2 Look

Find the word that is different:

a) school, hotel, mosque, park, airport, palace, hospital.
b) apple, orange, fruit, banana, watermelon, lemon.
c) teacher, doctor, nurse, job, secretary, driver, mechanic.
d) who, where, how, that, what.
e) thirsty, hungry, tired, sandwich, cold, happy, hot.
f) Qatar, Saudi Arabia, Egyptian, Jordan, Tunisia, Yemen.

3 Numbers

Write the numbers.

35	______________	58	______________
39	______________	59	______________
46	______________	60	______________
48	______________	63	______________
51	______________	67	______________

4 Match

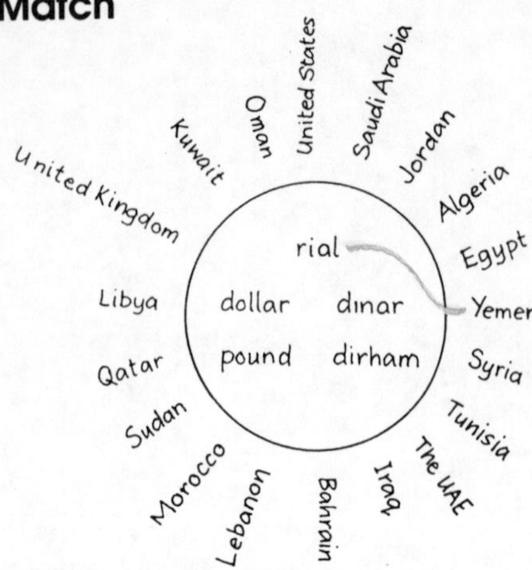

Look!

It's a car. It's beautiful.	It's a **beautiful car.**
They're dates. They're sweet.	They're **sweet dates.**

5 Write

a) They're houses. They're old.
They're ____________________

b) They're watches. They're expensive.
They're ____________________

c) They're new. They're drivers.
____

d) They're doctors. They're very good.
____

e) They're apricots. They're Egyptian.
____

6 Read

Ask and answer.

How much are the dates?
How much are ...?

They're 20 dirhams a kilo.
They're ...

Streets and roads

1 Write

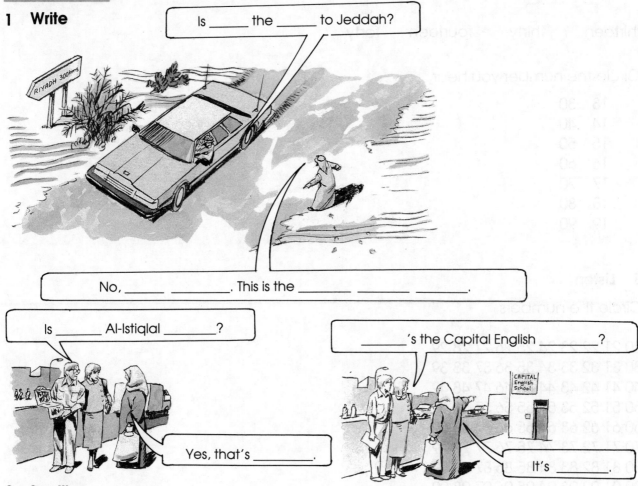

Is ______ the ______ to Jeddah?

No, ______ ______. This is the ______ ______ ______.

Is ______ Al-Istiqlal ______?

Yes, that's ______.

______'s the Capital English ______?

It's ______.

2 Spelling

Match the words.

station staiton, station, staytion, stashon, staition
garage garage, grage, garag, garige, garije
problem broblem, probelem, prablem, broplem, problem
orange oringe, orange, orinj, ornge, ornige,
street streat, street, stret, stireet, straet
road rode, road, raod, roade, rood
petrol peterol, betrol, beterel, petril, petrol

3 Match

Match the words with opposite meanings.

here
full
sweet
hot
there
late
early
far
near
empty
sour
cold.

4 Listen and say

thirteen thirty fourteen forty

Circle the number you hear.

13 30
14 40
15 50
16 60
17 70
18 80
19 90

5 Listen

Circle the numbers.

20 21 22 23 24 25 26 27 28 29
30 31 32 33 34 35 36 37 38 39
40 41 42 43 44 45 46 47 48 49
50 51 52 53 54 55 56 57 58 59
60 61 62 63 64 65 66 67 68 69
70 71 72 73 74 75 76 77 78 79
80 81 82 83 84 85 86 87 88 89
90 91 92 93 94 95 96 97 98 99

6 Numbers

Write these numbers:

71 ______________________
74 ______________________
76 ______________________
85 ______________________
88 ______________________
89 ______________________
92 ______________________
93 ______________________
97 ______________________
100 ______________________

7 Punctuation (', . ?) and capital letters

Write these sentences with punctuation and capital letters.

the capital english school is in al-istiqlal street it is not far from the market next to the school is a new bank the bank of the arabian gulf

____

____

____

8 Crossword

Across →

1

3 Where's … market?
4 nine + five = …
6 This is … new car.

7

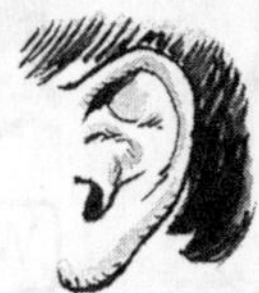

9 Your grandfather is very …

Down ↓

1 thirty-three + seventeen = …
2

3 "Who's that?" "Who?" "That man, …"
5 She's a …

6 He's a …

8 How much … this jacket?
10 "I'm hungry." "Have … apple."
11 How … you spell your name?
12 Excuse …, where's the Meridian Hotel?

Unit 5 What's it like?

Lesson 1 That's mine!

1 Write

Look at the table.

It's	my your his her our their	suitcase.

Write **my**, **your**, **his**, **her**, **our**, **their** in the spaces.

What's _____ name, please?
I'm Tom Brown.
These are my friends, Ahmed and Samia, and this is _____ daughter.
What's _____ name?
Muna.
This is my uncle.
_____ name's Tawfiq.
RECEPTION
Is this _____ room?
Yes, that's right.
Where's _____ passport?

2 Spelling

Match the words.

black	blick, belack, bleck, black, balck
red	rid, red, raid, read, reed
white	wite, white, wait, whiyet, whiet
blue	bleu, belu, blue, below, blew
brown	brawn, barown, browen, brown, brewn
green	grin, gren, grean, green, gareen
like	laik, lake, laek, like, liyk
mine	mine, main, mien, mane, miyn

3 Write

Write **my**, **mine**, **your**, **yours** in the spaces.

A: Excuse me. I think this is _____ seat.
B: No, it isn't. That's _____ seat. There.
A: No. That's ______. This is ______.
B: Oh. Sorry.

Look!

It's a red apple.	They're red apples.
The apple is red.	**The apples are red.**

4 Write

Look at exercise 6 on pages 91-92. Write sentences about the pictures, like this:

The ... is The ... are	red. blue. black. green. white. brown. yellow.

5 Read and write

My car is five years old.
It's a Toyota pick-up.
It's blue and white.

My brother's car is new.
It's a white Mercedes.

I don't have a car.

Our car is a red Datsun.
It's eight years old.

Write about a car. What's it like?

____

____

6 Read

Read the advertisements.

FOR SALE
Datsun 1.6 litre
1992 model. New brakes.
Excellent condition.
Only 20,000 dhms
Telephone : 756-3398

FOR SALE
Mitsubishi pick-up
Three years old
Only 3,000 kilometres
Very good condition
Price: 2500 JD
Tel: 265-892

A BARGAIN!
A Nissan Patrol for sale.
White and brown.
4-wheel drive.
1986 model. 50,000 km.
Good condition.
Price: OR 1100 o.n.o.
Phone: Salem 943-543
Ext 65

Now write an advertisement for a car.

Look ... half and half.
This is mine and that's yours.

Lesson 2 Whose is this?

1 Write

2 Spelling

Find the colours.

a) lube ________ b) clabk ________

c) owleyl ________ d) enreg ________

e) wonrb ________ f) tewih ________

g) dre ________

3 Spelling

Find the words. Write : **a, e, i, o, u**.

a) w h __ s __ e) h __ n d b __ g

b) s __ __ t c __ s __ f) r __ __ m

c) t __ c k __ t g) k __ y s

d) m __ n __ y h) p __ s s p __ r t

4 Write

Write **they're**, **there**, or **their** in the spaces.

a) Where's my book?

It's ________. Look!

b) Where are Abdullah and Mohammad from?

I think ________ from Saudi Arabia.

c) Where are Tom and Mary?

They are in ________ room.

5 Match

Match the question and the answer.

a)	Who is that?	1)	It's a new bank.
b)	Where's your hotel?	2)	I'm tired!
c)	How much is that?	3)	It's my brother's.
d)	What is that?	4)	39.
e)	How old are you?	5)	That's my cousin, Bashir.
f)	Whose bicycle is that?	6)	Near the market.
g)	How are you?	7)	Five dinars.

6 Punctuation (' , . ?) and capital letters

Write out these sentences with punctuation and capital letters.

a) whose is that ______________________________

b) it isnt mine ______________________________

c) its samiras ______________________________

d) thats my brothers car ______________________________

e) is this yours ______________________________

f) theyre ahmeds keys ______________________________

7 Read

Write the names **Ahmed**, **Ali**, **Bashir** and **Waleed** on the doors.

Bashir's room is next to Waleed's room. Ali's room is next to Ahmed's room, but it isn't near Bashir's room. Ahmed's room is next to Waleed's room and it's next to Ali's room. It isn't next to Bashir's room.

Lesson 3 She's got green eyes

1 Write

Look!
What's the time?
It's ten o'clock.

2 Ask and answer

What's the time? **It's ... o'clock.**

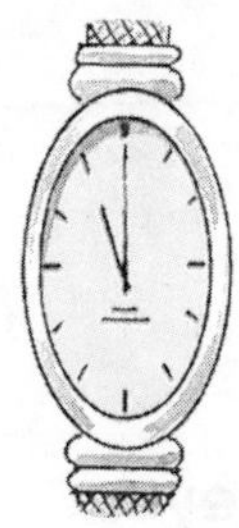

3 Spelling

Match the words.

fair	fare, fair, fiar, fire, fear
grey	grey, griy, garey, girey, grai
quite	quait, quiet, qjte, quite, qwite
very	vary, veri, vry, very, vairy
beard	berd, beard, beerd, baerd, bread
moustache	mustache, moustache, mustashe, moustach, mostache
thin	then, than, thain, thine, thin,
beautiful	beatiful, beautifull, beutiful, beautiful, beatful

4 Write

This is my brother. He is tall. **My brother is tall.**

a) This is my son. He is quite tall.

____

b) This is my sister. She's got brown hair and brown eyes.

____

c) This is my friend, Ahmed. He has got a beard and a moustache.

____

d) This is my grandfather. He's got grey hair.

____

e) This my daughter. She's eight years old.

____

5 Write

Write in the full form.

We're hungry.	**We are hungry**.
He's happy.	**He is happy**.
I'm not thirsty.	**I am not thirsty**.
He's got brown eyes.	**He has got brown eyes**.

a) They're from Saudi Arabia. ______________________________

b) She's got black hair. ______________________________

c) He isn't thirsty. ______________________________

d) She's a teacher. ______________________________

e) Where's he from? ______________________________

d) He's got a beard. ______________________________

g) What's it like? ______________________________

h) He's a clerk in a bank. ______________________________

i) We aren't from Egypt. ______________________________

j) It's a nice hotel. ______________________________

Look!

He's She's	tall. short. thin. fat.

He's She's	got	blue green brown black	eyes.

He's She's	got	brown long short blonde fair	black grey	hair.

He's got	a beard. a moustache.

He's got no hair. He's **bald**.

6 Read and match

1) My aunt's name is Suhair. She's not very tall. She's got long black hair and brown eyes. She's quite old, but she's very thin.
2) Peter Roberts is quite tall. He's a teacher in a secondary school in Oman. He's got fair hair and blue eyes. He's got a big moustache, too.
3) My brother's name is Tariq. He's big and quite fat. He's got short black hair and a moustache. He's not very handsome.
4) Ann Hobson is a secretary in a bank. She's quite small and thin. She's got long blonde hair and blue eyes. She's quite pretty.

7 Write

Write about two people you know.

Lesson 4 How many?

1 Write

Complete the table.

	singular	*plural*
s	a son a girl a house	sons ________ ________
es	a box a watch a sandwich	box**es** ________ ________
ies	a baby a country a city	bab**ies** ________ ________
Irregular	a child a man a woman	________ men women

2 How many?

six boxes ________ ________ ________ ________

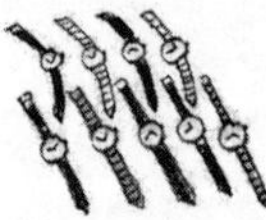

________ ________ ________ ________

3 Questions

Put the words in order.

a) brother / 's / like / what / your ? ________________

b) many / got / you / children / have / how ? ________________

c) married / you / are ? ________________

d) ticket / this / whose / is ? ________________

e) your / old / daughter / how / is ? ________________

f) time / 's / the / what ? ________________

Now match with the answers.

1 I haven't got any.
2 He's tall and quite handsome.
3 Six o'clock.
4 It's mine.
5 Two and a half.
6 No, I'm single.

4 Spelling

Match the words.

children	childeren, chilidren, children, childrn, childerin
women	wmen, woman, wemen, women, womin
baby	beby, bebi, babi, babby, baby,
daughter	daughter, dauhgter, duaghter, daughtr, doughter
son	sun, san, son, sen, soon
married	maried, marryed, marred, married, marride
single	sangle, single, singel, snigle, singal
month	manth, month, monthe, munth, moneth

5 Write

Write these words **a, the, in, got, old, is, is, children** in the spaces.

My friend Khalid ____ from Cairo. He's Egyptian. He's ____ clerk in the Ministry of Labour. He's ____ a flat in Dokki ____ Cairo. He's got a wife and two ____________, a boy and a girl. The boy ____ three years old and ______ girl is eighteen months _____

6 Read and write

My friend Samia is Omani. She's a student at the Sultan Qaboos University.

She's twenty-three years old. She's married but she hasn't got any children.

Her husband is an officer in the army.

Write about a friend.

Where is he/she from? What's his/her job? Is he/she married or single? How many children has he/she got?

My friend ______________________________

____

____

____

7 Crossword

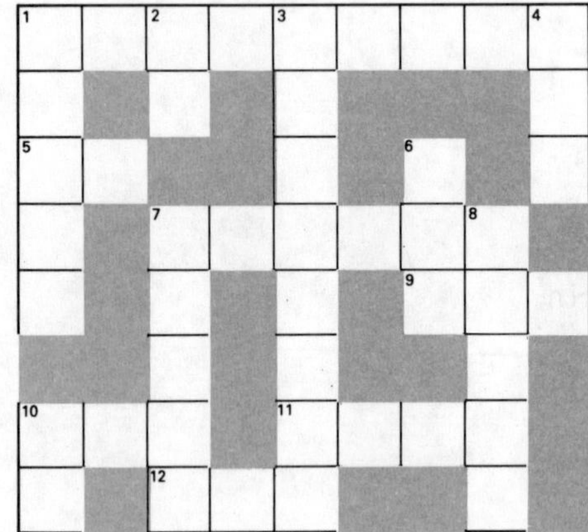

Across →

1 

5 "Tea … coffee?" "Tea, please."

7 The colour of lemons.

9 "What's that?"
"It's … Great Pyramid of Giza."

10 Those are … seats, not yours!

11 

12 "How many children have you got?"
"Three – two daughters and one …"

Down ↓

1 Waleed's not tall. He's …

2 "I'm sorry I'm late."
"… doesn't matter."

3 

4 Twenty-three–seventeen = …

6 I'm hungry. Have you … any dates?

7 Salah's 26 … old.

8 "… ticket is this?"
"It's mine!"

10 Jamala's a clerk in the Ministry … Labour.

Unit 6 Where is it?

Lesson 1 The second door on the right

1 Write

______ ______ Ministry of Foreign Affairs, please?
Go ______ this ______. It's ______ ______ left.

2 Spelling

Match the words.

ground gruond, garound, ground, graund, geround
first frist, first, firest, fairst, ferst
second secand, seckond, scond, seconed, second
third thaird, third, therd, thired, tird
left left, lift, laft, lefit, letf
right rihgt, raight, right, rigth, righte
stairs sters, stiars, stares, stairs, steers
broken browken, broken, brokin, beroken, brokn
office office, ofice, offise offis, offiec

3 Match

Go along the corridor. Go up the stairs. Go down the stairs. Stop. Wait.

______ ______ ______ ______ ______

______ ______ ______ ______ ______

4 Write

Write **a**, **an**, **the** or **(-)** in the spaces.

a) Excuse me. Where's _____ airport?

b) "What's that building over there?"
"It's _____ hotel."

c) These are _____ fresh dates.

d) It's _____ third door on _____ right.

e) It's _____ beautiful palace.

f) They're _____ expensive cars.

g) It's _____ old house.

h) His office is on _____ fifth floor.

i) Hassan's from _____ Egypt.

5 Read and write

Read about ITC. Write these places on the plan:

the canteen, the computer room, the lift, the reception, the manager's office, the toilets, the secretary's office, the stairs, the photocopying room.

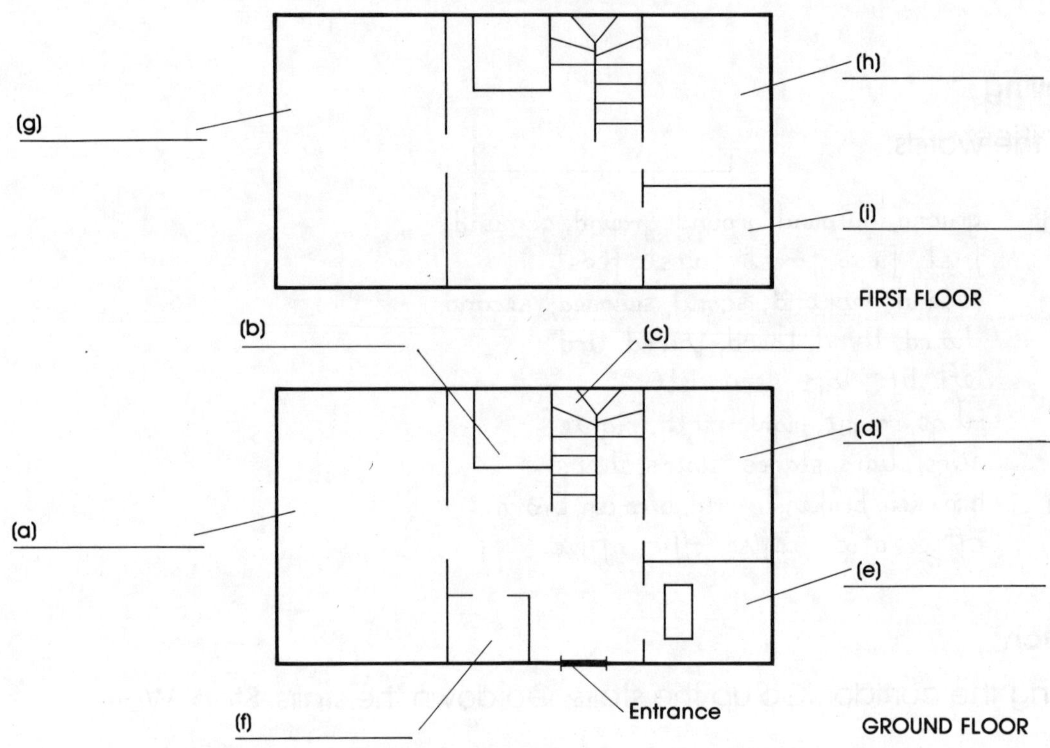

These are the offices of ITC, an engineering company. The reception is on the ground floor next to the entrance, on the right. The photocopying room is also on the right next to the stairs. The lift is next to the stairs. The canteen is on the left next to the lift. The toilets are near the entrance, on the left. The manager's office is on the first floor near the stairs. The secretary's office is a small room. It is next to the manager's office on the right. The computer room is on the left.

6 Ask and answer

Where's the ...?	**It's**	**on the ... floor.**
Where are the ...?	**They're**	**near the ...**
		next to the ...

Ask about **the canteen, the reception, the manager's office, the secretary's office, the toilets, the computer room, the stairs, the lift, the photocopying room.**

7 Write

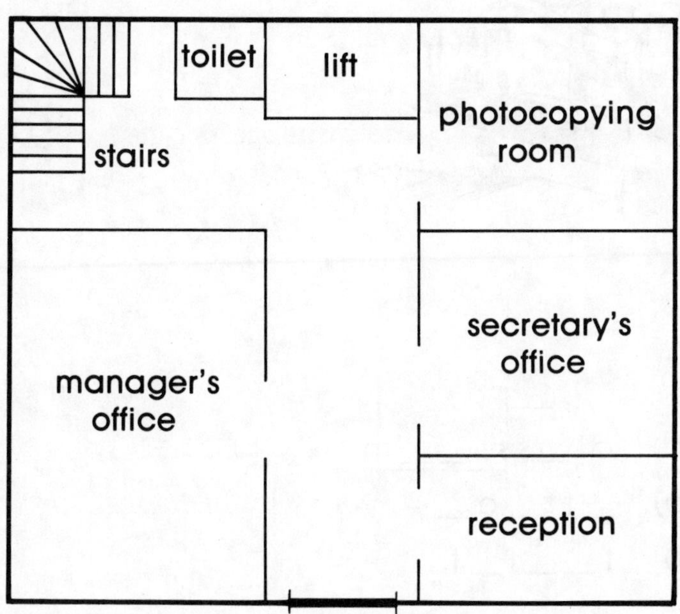

These are the offices of ABC Ltd. The reception is on

the right near the entrance.

Lesson 2 Latifa's village

1 Write

______ there ______ good restaurants near here?
Yes, ______ ______ a nice restaurant ______ to the bus station.

2 Spelling

Spell these rooms. Write: **a**, **e**, **i**, **o**, **u**.

a) k _ t ch _ n,

b) s _ t t _ n g r _ _ m

c) b _ d r _ _ m

d) c l _ s s r _ _ m

e) _ f f _ c _

f) t _ _ l _ t

Match with the pictures.

1 ______________________

4 ______________________

2 ______________________

5 ______________________

3 ______________________

6 ______________________

3 Write

Write **on** or **in**.

a) Jeddah is ____ Saudi Arabia.

b) My house is ____ the middle of the village.

c) Her office is ____ the third floor.

d) Lutfi is a clerk ____ a bank.

e) The photocopying room is ____ the right.

f) The Montazah Palace is ____ Alexandria.

4 Write

Write **am**, **is** or **are**.

a) They ____ from Saudi Arabia.

b) Nadia ____ an English teacher

c) There ____ two hotels on the right.

d) Whose car ____ this?

e) Where ____ you from?

f) I ____ sorry.

f) There ____ a toilet next to the lift.

g) We ____ hungry. ____ there a restaurant near here?

h) ____ I late?

5 Look and say

1) **Student B**. Write the names of the buildings.

________ ________ ________ ________

________ ________ ________

2) **Student B**. Talk about this street.

There is …
There are …

next to
between … and
on the left/right.

6 Write

There is a hospital on _____ left. Next ____ the hospital there _____ two houses. On the right __________ is a small __________. In the __________ of the picture there is a __________ __________ the garage and the hotel __________ is a bank.

Write about this street.

There is a mosque on the left. Next to the mosque

____

____

____

____

____

7 Word puzzle

Find the places in a city.

One is done. Find 11 more.

A T M E S H O P B Z
I H O T E L X G A H
R E S T A U R A N T
P A Q P B M O R K U
O V U A P A L A C E
R J E R F K U G A O
T A S K E D R E I K
B U S S T A T I O N
D M I M A R K E T A
F H O S P I T A L R

Lesson 3 Can I speak to Mrs Roberts?

1 Write

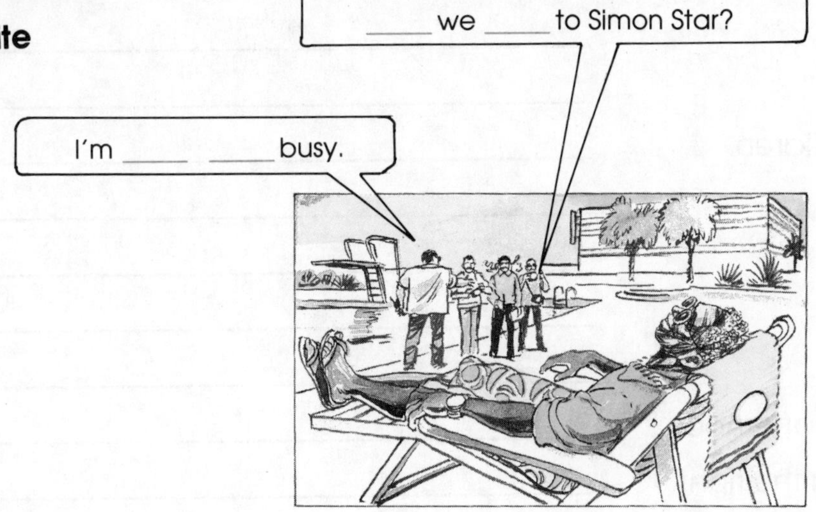

2 Write

Find the days of the week.

a) DUNSYA ____________
b) ESDTAUY ____________
c) DEDSEANWY ____________
d) NODAMY ____________
e) AFIDYR ____________
f) TURSYHDA ____________
g) SAYAUDRT ____________

Now write them in order.

____

____

3 Write

Put the sentences in order.

a) His secretary's out.
b) OK. I'll phone again this afternoon.
c) Can I speak to his secretary?
d) Good afternoon. Can I speak to the manager?
e) Goodbye.
f) Gulf Air. Good afternoon.
g) I'm sorry, he's busy.

1 ____

2 ____

3 ____

4 ____

5 ____

6 ____

7 ____

4 Write

Write these sentences in their full form.

a) He's busy. ____________________

b) That's Gary's office. ____________________

c) Mary's got three children. ____________________

d) I'm not hungry. ____________________

e) We're from Syria. ____________________

f) I've got a house. ____________________

g) She isn't here today. ____________________

h) I'll phone again this afternoon. ____________________

i) There's a garage on the right. ____________________

5 Punctuation and capital letters

Write out these sentences with punctuation and capital letters.

a) tomorrow is saturday ____________________

b) go along the corridor ____________________

c) wheres the managers office ____________________

d) theres a bank on the right ____________________

e) is today sunday or monday ____________________

f) can i speak to mrs brown please ____________________

6 Listen and write

Listen to the hotel manager. Where are these places?

a) small restaurant
b) large restaurant
c) room 418
d) coffee shop
e) shops
f) reception
g) room 235

7 Dictation

Listen and write.

____

____

____

____

Lesson 4 Peter's classroom

1 Match

Match the prepositions:

up, down, along, next to, near, between, in, on.

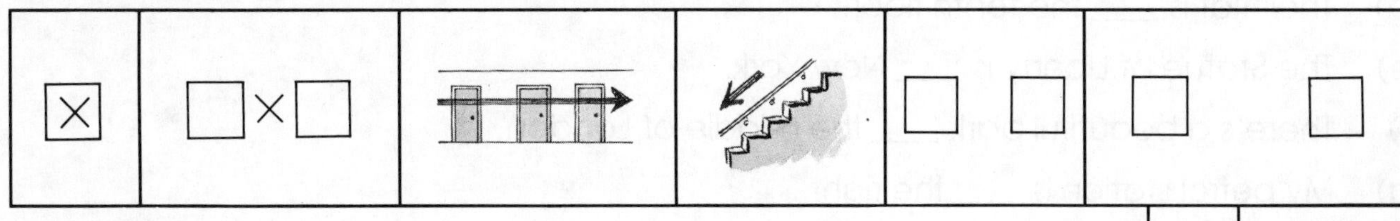

2 Spelling

Double letters. Put the double letters in these words.

Example: corridor

a) si_ _ing room
b) mi_ _le
c) o_ _ice
d) ca_ _e_ _e
e) vi_ _age
f) cla_ _room
g) tomo_ _ow
h) so_ _y

3 Spelling

Match the words.

hundred	handred, hundred, hundered, handrid, hundrid
thousand	thuosand, tousand, thousant, thousand, thousend
cupboard	cuboard, cupboard, cubboard, cupbaord, cupbroad
table	taible, taeble, table, tabel, tayble
window	wandow, window, windowe, wndow, waindow
desk	desk, dask, disk, deks, daks
door	doer, door, dore, dower, dare
wall	wal, well, wall, woll, wale
blackboard	blackboard, bleckboard, blakboard, blackbord, blackbroad
chair	chair, chiar, chare, chere, chaer

4 Listen and write

Numbers

387											

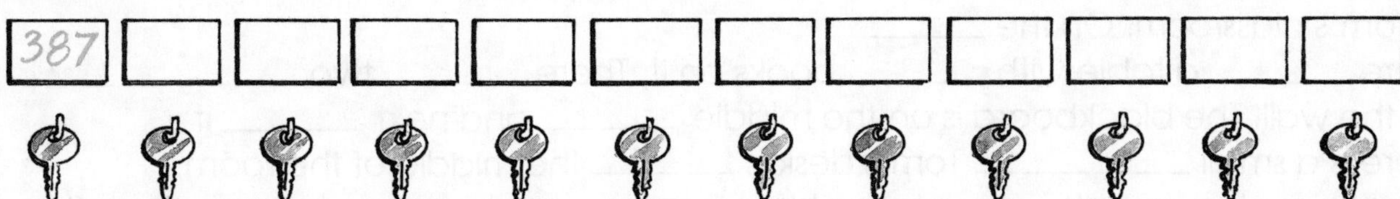

Now write out the numbers in full.

5 Write

Write **in** or **on** in the spaces.

a) Are there any desks ____ the room?

b) Where's my book? It's ____ the table.

c) There's a house ____ the left.

d) Their flat is ____ the tenth floor.

e) The Statue of Liberty is ____ New York.

f) There's a beautiful park ____ the middle of London.

g) My petrol station is ____ the right.

h) There's a beautiful picture ____ the wall.

i) Where's my passport? It's ____ your handbag.

6 Questions

Put the words in order.

a) you / I / can / help? ____________________

b) office / is / Mr Saeedi's / please / where? ____________________

c) station / village / in / is / a / there / the / petrol? ____________________

d) the / there / room / how / chairs / in / many / are? ____________________

e) like / is / house / what / your? ____________________

f) speak / Sarah / I / please / can / to? ____________________

7 Read and write

Tom is a teacher at the Capital English school. This is Tom's classroom.

Complete the paragraph.

There are ten desks and chairs in Tom's classroom. On the ________ there ________ a table with ________ books on it. There ________ two ________ on the wall. The blackboard is on the middle ________ and next ________ it there is a small ________. Tom's desk is ________ the middle of the room. ________ is a cassette recorder on his ________ and a ________ on the left. On the right there is a large ________ and next to it there ________ a door.

8 Crossword

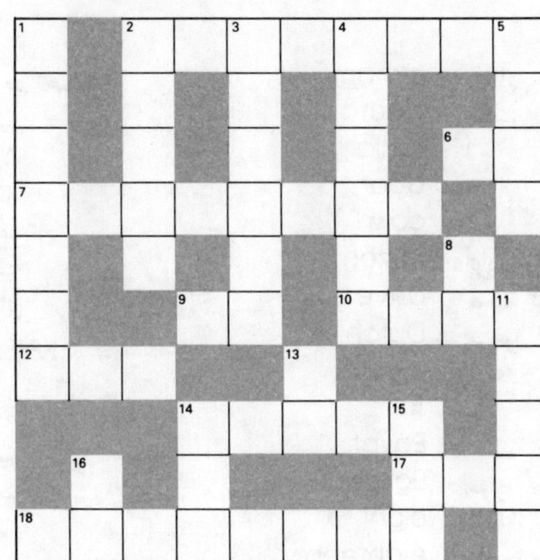

Across →

2 1000 = a ...
6 The traffic light is green. ...!
7

9 My sister and I are from Doha. ... are Qatari.
10 Right or ...?
12 I'm sorry. Mr Jones is ... here.
14 10th
17 We are from Cairo . ... nationality is Egyptian.
18 Today is Sunday. ... is Monday.

Down ↓

1

2 ... are two airports in this city.
3 "Where's the manager's ... please?"
"It's the second room on the right."
4 That's a primary ...
5

8 There's a table in the middle ... the room.
11 First, second,...
13 Our flat is ... the sixth floor.
14 Aleppo is in Syria. Damascus is in Syria ...
15 ... many rooms are there is this hotel?
16 "Where's the lift?"
"Over there. Next ... the stairs."

Appendix قائمة كلمات

1 wordlist

A

about	حوالى
actor	ممثل
afternoon	بعد الظهر
airline	خط جوي
airport	مطار
Algeria	الجزائر (البلد)
Algerian	جزائري
all right	وهو كذلك
along	على طول – بموازاة
America	أمريكا
American	أمريكي
and	و – للإضافة
answer	إجابة – يجيب
any	أي
apple	تفاحة
apricot	مشمش
Arab	شخص عربي
ask	يسأل
aspirin	أسبرين
atlas	أطلس
aunt	عمة أو خالة

B

baby	طفل رضيع
bad	سيئ
bag	شنطة – حقيبة
Bahrain	البحرين
Bahraini	بحريني
bald	أصلع
banana	إصبع موز
bank	بنك – ضفة النهر
basketball player	لاعب كرة السلة
bathroom	حمام (حجرة)
battery	بطارية
beard	لحية – ذقن
beautiful	جميل
bedroom	حجرة نوم
between	بين – وبين
bicyle	عجلة
big	كبير
black	أسود
blonde	شقراء
blue	أزرق
book	كتاب
box	صندوق
boy	ولد
brakes	فرامل
British	بريطاني
broken	مكسور
brother	أخ
brown	بني
building	مبنى – بناية
bus	أتوبيس
bus station	محطة أتوبيس
busy	مشغول
bye-bye	وداعا – إلى اللقاء

C

cab	سيارة أجرة
cable	برقية
camera	كاميرا – آلة تصوير
can I ...?	هل يمكن ... ؟
canteen	مقصف
car	سيارة
cassette	كاسيت
cassette recorder	جهاز تسجيل
chair	كرسي
cheap	رخيص
child	طفل
children (pl.)	أطفال
city	مدينة
classroom	فصل (حجرة دراسة)
clerk	كاتب (موظف)
clutch	دبرياج (القابض)
coffee	بن – قهوة
coffee shop	مقهى – محل القهوة
cold	بارد
come	يأتي
come on!	يتقدم – يتطور
comma	فاصلة
company	شركة
computer	كومبيوتر (الحاسب الآلي)
corridor	طرقة – ممر – دهليز
country	بلد
cousin	ابن العم
crossword	كلمات متقاطعة
cupboard	دولاب
customs	عادات

D

date	تاريخ
daughter	ابنة
day	يوم
desk	مكتب
dinar	الدينار (عملة)
dining room	حجرة المائدة
diploma	دبلوم – شهادة
dirham	درهم (عملة)
doctor	طبيب – دكتور
dollar	دولار
door	باب
down	أسفل
dozen	دستة
driver	سائق
Dutch	هولندي

E

Egypt	مصر
Egyptian	مصري
eight	ثمانية
eighteen	ثمانية عشر
eighty	ثمانون
eleven	إحدى عشرة
Emirati	إماراتي (مواطن من الإمارات)
empty	فارغ
engineering	هندسة
England	إنجلترا
English	إنجليزي
entrance	مدخل
evening	مساء
exchange	يتبادل
exclamation mark	علامة تعجب
Excuse me	أ تسمح لي (لو سمحت)
expensive	غال
express	سريع
eyes	عيون

F

fair	جميل
famliy	عائلة
famliy name	اسم العائلة
fat	سمين
father	أب
fifteen	خمسة عشر
fifth	الخامس
fifty	خمسون
film	فيلم
fine	جميل – ناعم – حساس
first	أول
first name	الاسم الأول
five	خمسة
floor	أرضية
form	شكل
forty	أربعون
four	أربعة
fourteen	أربعة عشر
fourth	الرابع

France	فرنسا
freezer	مجمد
French	فرنسي
fresh	طازج
Friday	يوم الجمعة
friend	صديق
from	من
fruit	فاكهة
full	كامل
full stop	نقطة – علامة وقف

G

gallon	جالون
garage	جاراج
gas	غاز
German	ألماني
Germany	ألمانيا
girl	بنت
Go!	اذهب !
Go along ...	يتقدم – يرافق
goal	هدف
good	حسن
Good afternoon	تحية بعد الظهر
Good evening	مساء الخير
Good luck!	حظا سعيداً
Good morning	صباح الخير
Good night	تصبح على خير
grandfather	جد
grandmother	جدة
green	أخضر
grey	رمادي
ground	أرض

H

hair	شعر
handle	يد
handsome	أنيق
happy	سعيد
Happy Birthday!	عيد ميلاد سعيداً
Have a ...	ليكن ...
Hello!	أهلاً
here	هنا
Hi!	مرحباً
Holland	هولندا
horn	بوق
hospital	مستشفى
hot	حار
hotel	لوكاندة – فندق
house	بيت
How are you?	كيف حالك ؟
How do you do?	كيف حالك ؟
How many ...?	كم (للعدد) ؟
How much ...?	كم (للثمن) ؟
a hundred	مائة
hungry	جوعان
husband	زوج

I

ice-cream	أيس كريم
immigration	هجرة
in	في
in the middle	في المنتصف
inch	بوصة
Iraq	العراق
Iraqi	عراقي

J

jack	رجل (بحار – نوتي) – رافعة (كوريك)
jacket	جاكتة
Japan	اليابان
Japanese	ياباني
jeans	بنطلون جينز
job	وظيفة – مهنة
Jordan	الأردن
Jordanian	أردني
just a minute	دقيقة لو سمحت

K

karate	كاراتيه
ketchup	الكاتشاب
key	مفتاح
kilo	كيلوجرام
kilometre	كيلومتر
king	ملك
kitchen	المطبخ (حجرة المطبخ)
Kuwait	الكويت
Kuwaiti	كويتي

L

late	متأخر
Lebanese	لبناني
Lebanon	لبنان
left	شمال
lemon	ليمون
lemonade	شراب الليمونادة
Libya	ليبيا
Libyan	ليبي
lift	مصعد (أسانسير)
listen	يستمع
long	طويل
look	ينظر
lorry	لوري

M

man	رجل
manager	مدير
market	سوق
married	متزوج
match	مباراة – يضاهي – يماثل
mechanic	ميكانيكي
middle	وسط
mine	ملكي
ministry	وزارة
Ministry of Foreign Affairs	وزارة الخارجية
Ministry of Labour	وزارة العمل
minute	دقيقة
mirror	مرآة
Monday	يوم الاثنين
month	شهر
morning	صباح
Moroccan	مغربي – مراكشي
Morocco	المغرب
mosque	مسجد
mother	أم
moustache	شارب
Mr	السيد
Mrs	السيدة
music	موسيقى
my	ملكي (ضمير)
My name's ...	اسمي .....

N

name	الاسم
nationality	الجنسية
near	قريب
new	جديد
next to	ملاصق لـ
nice	لطيف
night	ليل
nine	تسعة
nineteen	تسعة عشر
ninety	تسعون
ninth	التاسع
no	لا
Not bad	ليس سيئا
number	عدد
nurse	ممرضة

O

o'clock	الساعة
office	مكتب
officer	ضابط
offside	خارج النطاق
Oh!	آه

old	قديم – كبير في السن
Oman	عمان
Omani	عماني
on	على
on the left	في الشمال
on the right	في اليمين
on the ... floor	في الطابق...
one	واحد
orange	برتقالة
out	خارج
over there	هناك
P	
page	صفحة
palace	قصر
Palestinian	فلسطيني
park	منتزه – موقف سيارات
passport	جواز سفر
pen	قلم
people	ناس
petrol	بنزين
petrol station	محطة بنزين
phone	صوت
photocopying	ماكينة تصوير
picture	صورة
please	من فضلك
pleased	مسرور
pleased to meet you	مسرور لرؤيتك
policeman	رجل شرطة
politician	رجل سياسي
pretty	جميل
primary school	مدرسة ابتدائية
pull	يجذب
puncture	ثقب في إطار السيارة
punctuation	علامات الترقيم
push	يدفع
Q	
Qatar	قطر
Qatari	قطري
queen	ملكة
queue	طابور
quite	تماماً
R	
radio	راديو
read	يقرأ
reception	استقبال
red	أحمر
rest	يستريح
restaurant	مطعم
rice	أرز

right	صواب
road	طريق
room	حجرة
royal palace	القصر الملكي
S	
salad	سلاطة
sandwich	سندوتش
say	يقول
Saturday	يوم السبت
Saudi Arabia	السعودية (العربية)
Saudi	سعودي
school	مدرسة
seat	مقعد
second	ثان
secretary	سكرتير(ة)
seven	سبعة
seventeen	سبعة عشر
seventh	السابع
seventy	سبعون
shampoo	شامبو
shop	محل – متجر
short	قصير
single	أعزب – بمفرده
sister	أخت
sitting room	حجرة الجلوس
six	ستة
sixteen	ستة عشر
sixth	السادس
sixty	ستون
small	صغير
So am I	وهكذا أكون أنا
son	ابن
Sorry!	آسف
spaceman	رجل فضاء
speak	يتكلم
spell	يتهجى
spelling	التهجي
stairs	السلالم
station	المحطة
stereo	ستريو
stop	يتوقف – موقف – محطة
street	شارع
student	طالب
Sudan	السودان
Sudanese	سوداني
suitcase	شنطة ملابس (حقيبة)
sun	الشمس
Sunday	الأحد
sweet	حلوى
Syria	سوريا
Syrian	سوري

T	
table	ترابيزة – منضدة
taxi	تاكسي – سيارة أجرة
tea	شاي
teacher	معلم – مدرس
telephone	التليفون
telephone number	رقم التليفون
ten	عشرة
tenth	العاشر
thanks	شكرا
thank you very much	شكرا جزيلا
that	ذاك
that's all right	هذا سليم
their	ملكيتهم
theirs	خاص بهم
there	هناك
There is ...	يوجد (للمفرد)
There are ...	يوجد (للجمع)
these	هؤلاء
thin	نحيف – رفيع
thing	شيء
third	الثالث
thirsty	عطشان
thirteen	ثلاثة عشر
thirty	ثلاثون
this	هذا
those	هؤلاء
thousand	ألف
three	ثلاثة
Thursday	الخميس
time	وقت
today	اليوم
toilets	دورات مياه
tomorrow	غدا
too	أيضا
tree	شجرة
truck	عربة نقل (سيارة)
Tuesday	الثلاثاء
Tunisia	تونس
Tunisian	تونسي
twelve	اثنا عشر
twenty	عشرون
two	اثنان
U	
umbrella	مظلة (شمسية)
uncle	عم أو خال
The United Arab Emirates	دولة الإمارات العربية المتحدة
The United Kingdom	المملكة المتحدة
The United States of America	الولايات المتحدة الأمريكية

up أعلى
upstairs في الطابق العلوي

V
very جدا
video فيديو
villa فيلا
visa فيزا (تأشيرة)

W
wait ينتظر
wall حائط
watermelon بطيخ
Wednesday الأربعاء
week أسبوع
What? ماذا ؟
What's your name? ما اسمك ؟
What's the time? ما الساعة ؟
Where...? أين ؟
Where are you from? من أين أنت ؟
white أبيض
Who ...? من ... ؟
Who's that? من هذا ؟
wife زوجة
window نافذة
workshop ورشة
write يكتب

X
X-ray أشعة إكس

Y
yacht يخت
year سنة
yellow أصفر
Yemen اليمن
Yemeni يمني
yes نعم
young صغير

Z
zebra حمار وحشي
zero صفر

Acknowledgements

The Publishers are grateful to the following for their permission to reproduce photographs:

Al-Quds al Arabi Publishing for pages 42 centre middle and 134 top middle left; Barnaby's Picture Library for page 68 bottom right, Camera Press for pages 42 bottom, 134 bottom middle left, 134 bottom middle and 134 bottom far right: J. Allen Cash Photo Library for page 68 bottom left and centre; Isreal Government Tourist Office for page 68 top left; The Kobal Collection for page 134 top right and top middle; London Tourist Office for page 68 top far right; Popperfoto for page 42 top left, top middle, centre left and centre right; Sherlock Holmes Reference Collection for page 134 bottom far left and George Stamkoski Media for pages 42 top right and 134 top far left.

We are unable to trace the copyright holder of the photograph on page 68 top middle right and would welcome any information enabling us to do so.

2 Grammatical terms

small letter b حرف صغير
capital letter B حرف كبير

word كلمة
sentence جملة
paragraph فقرة

bag الشنطة (الحقيبة)
This is my bag. هذه حقيبتي

question سؤال
question word كلمة استفهام

Are you from Qatar? هل أنت من قطر ؟
where? what? who? etc. أين ؟ ماذا ؟ من ؟ إلخ

singular مفرد
plural جمع

a car سيارة
cars سيارات

regular plural جمع عادي
irregular plural جمع شاذ

car → cars سيارة – سيارات
man → men رجل – رجال

adjective صفة
verb فعل
preposition حرف جر

red, big, old, etc. أحمر ، كبير ، قديم ، الخ .
to be, to go, to have يكون ، يذهب ، يملك
up, down, etc. أعلى ، أسفل ، إلخ

abbreviation اختصار
BBC هيئة الإذاعة البريطانية

punctuation علامات ترقيم
- full stop . نقطة
- comma , فاصلة
- question mark ? علامة استفهام
- exclamation mark ! علامة تعجب
- apostrophe ' فاصلة علوية

spelling التهجي
Helo - × هالو
Hello - ✓ هالو

grammar القواعد
language اللغة